A Voice from the Civil Rights Era

A Voice from the Civil Rights Era

Frankye Regis

Voices of Twentieth-Century Conflict
Carol Schulz, Series Editor

Greenwood Press
Westport, Connecticut • London

Library of Congress Cataloging-in-Publication Data

Regis, Frankye V.
    A voice from the Civil Rights era / Frankye Regis.
        p. cm.—(Voices of twentieth-century conflict)
    Includes bibliographical references and index.
    ISBN 0–313–32998–2 (alk. paper)
    1. Regis, Frankye V.—Childhood and youth—Juvenile literature.
2. African American girls—Mississippi—Biography—Juvenile literature.
3. African Americans—Mississippi—Biography—Juvenile literature.   4.
African Americans—Civil rights—Mississippi—History—20th century—
Juvenile literature.   5. Civil rights movements—Mississippi—History—20th
century—Juvenile literature.   6. Mississippi—Race relations—Juvenile
literature.   7. Clinton Region (Miss.)—Biography—Juvenile literature.   8.
African Americans—Civil rights—Mississippi—History—20th century—
Study and teaching (Secondary)   9. Civil rights movements—Mississippi—
History—20th century—Study and teaching (Secondary)   10. Mississippi—
Race relations—Study and teaching (Secondary)   I. Title.   II. Series.
E185.97.R44A3   2004
323'.092—dc22   2004054385
[B]

British Library Cataloguing in Publication Data is available.

Library of Congress Catalog Card Number: 2004054385
ISBN: 0–313–32998–2

First published in 2004

Greenwood Press, 88 Post Road West, Westport, CT 06881
An imprint of Greenwood Publishing Group, Inc.
www.greenwood.com

Printed in the United States of America

The paper used in this book complies with the
Permanent Paper Standard issued by the National
Information Standards Organization (Z39.48–1984).

10 9 8 7 6 5 4 3 2 1

It's not easy being a mama,
when babies come like stair steps.
It's not easy being a mama,
when your dreams and aspirations die with your dead babies.
It's not easy being a mama,
with eight children pulling on your dress tail.
It's not easy being a mama,
when you have more children than food on the table.
It's not easy being a mama,
when the weight of the world lies on your breast.
It's not easy being a mama,
when you wear rags, so your children will have clothes for
    school.
It's not easy being a mama,
when the thought of death is the answer to all your problems.
It's not easy being a mama,
when you fear your children will grow up and leave you alone.
It's not easy being a mama.

Frankye Regis

Contents

Contents

To the Teacher

As a middle and high school history teacher, I have spent years trying to find books that excite students. As good as some textbooks can be, even the best among them provide more facts and statistics than engaging stories. Historical fiction sometimes fills the gap, but it is, after all, fiction. History needs to be vivid and alive if we are to capture the attention of students. That is the intention of the Voices of Twentieth-Century Conflict series.

The series focuses on significant periods and events of the twentieth century, e.g., the Holocaust and the Vietnam War. Each volume is a primary source that looks at a historical period through the eyes of one individual. Most of the stories in the series occurred when the authors were children and young adults. Through personal vignettes and reflections, they reveal the ways in which global events challenged their beliefs and changed their lives forever.

To create a context for each story, an introduction, a timeline, a glossary, and brief historical essays are included. And, of course, each volume includes photographs, maps, or other graphics that will engage young adult readers.

At the end of each book are questions and projects that encourage students to make connections between their own lives and the life of the author and that invite them to reflect on the universal themes raised in the text.

Most important, the stories in this series demonstrate clearly that we live in a global community, and that the choices each one of us makes can have profound consequences, not just for ourselves, but for everyone—even those we have yet to meet.

In an age when students require both critical thinking skills and historical perspective to make wise choices, the authors and I believe that this engaging and thought-provoking series will meet this crucial need.

Carol D. Schulz

Foreword

On the occasion of the fiftieth anniversary of *Brown v. Board of Education*, comedian, actor, author, and Doctor of Education Bill Cosby voiced his strong disapproval of young black males who glorify violence, disdain education, and demean traditional family life. Dr. Cosby harshly reprimanded them for failing to take advantage of the Supreme Court's assertion that "the doctrine of 'separate but equal' has no place" in our schools and our society.

Whether we agree with Dr. Cosby's accusation or believe that this harsh judgment is unwarranted and undeserved, it is clear from Frankye Regis' writings that generations of Southern blacks—men, women, and young people—have made tremendous sacrifices in order to fulfill the promise of integration.

In addition, despite the Supreme Court's words (monumentally obvious even in 1896, when a supremely racist Court created the idea of "separate but equal"), many people, both white and black, found that they had to continue, throughout the 1950s, 1960s, and 1970s, to make sacrifices to achieve equality. One could easily argue that although the laws supporting desegregation have certainly led to profound changes for the better, the gap between black and white America still exists. Recent Supreme Court rulings have allowed states to abandon plans for integration, and today, overall, schools are more segregated than they were in 1968. In fact, one-sixth of America's black students attend racially isolated schools. (Orfield and Frankenberg. "Where Are We Now?" *Teaching Tolerance.* Southern Poverty Law Center. Spring 2004.)

Although the time for sit-ins, bus boycotts, and freedom marches has passed, the struggle is not over. It is my fervent hope that this moving account of one black woman's experiences while growing up in rural Mississippi during the heart of the civil rights movement will inspire us all to pursue the fight for equality to its finish.

Carol D. Schulz

Preface

In this book, I explain the civil rights movement by focusing on my life growing up in rural, segregated Mississippi, and describing how a Southern legal system of racism and discrimination profoundly affected me, my family, and the entire black race. It was both painful and rewarding. I was shocked at how our government played a major role in oppressing blacks, but I was thrilled to learn that blacks never gave up the struggle for equality.

Throughout the years, people have differed on when they think the civil rights movement began. Some believe it began with the 1955 bus boycott in Montgomery, Alabama, and consider Rosa Parks the mother of the civil rights movement because her actions kicked off the yearlong boycott. Parks, a seamstress, sat on a segregated city bus and refused to give up her seat to a white man. She was arrested and jailed. At that time, the law required that a black person had to give up his or her seat in the black section in the back of city buses if all the seats for whites in the front were occupied.

I like to think that there were two civil rights movements—a historical one and a modern one, which started with Parks. The former movement dates back to 1619, when whites first brought blacks to this country as slaves. The degrading trans-Atlantic boat trips killed many Africans, who were transported against their will in chains to this young country as free labor. From the beginning, Africans tried to fight back, but it was impossible to stand up for themselves in an unfamiliar country where they couldn't speak the language. If a slave dared to escape, he or she was severely beaten or even killed to set an example for others who might have the same idea.

In my personal account of the civil rights movement, I weave in some background about slavery, the Reconstruction era, and Black Nationalism at the turn of the twentieth century, and how all of these set the stage for the modern civil rights movement.

While I was growing up in rural Mississippi, my parents kept me and my siblings isolated from the violence that reverberated during the Freedom Rides, when blacks and whites integrated interstate buses and were arrested and jailed in Southern states as soon as the Greyhound and Trailways buses pulled into the stations. We did not take part in Freedom Summer when mostly young white students came to Mississippi in droves and opened Freedom Schools for black children and helped blacks register to vote. Any black person who was associated with the voting campaign had visits from the Klu Klux Klan (KKK), and I assume my parents didn't want to wake up one morning with a cross burning in their front yard. But when the Voting Rights Act of 1965 was passed, my parents never failed to exercise their right to vote.

I talk about my experience in dilapidated Mississippi schools and how the state vehemently fought integration at all costs. My high school in Clinton, Mississippi, wasn't integrated until 1981— twenty-seven years after the U.S. Supreme Court ruled that segregated schools were illegal. Mississippi and other Southern states thumbed their noses at federal law and kept the segregated lifestyles that they thoroughly enjoyed.

Capturing the civil rights movement in a single book is a massive undertaking because there were so many people involved in numerous places around the country. Some events overlap and many went undocumented. Most of us have heard about heroes like Martin Luther King and Rosa Parks, but there were hundreds of regular people, just like you and me, who lost their lives and livelihoods in the struggle for freedom for all of us.

I wrap up the book with how life in Mississippi is today. I go back at least once a year to visit family there. I still call it home, and it feels like any other place I've lived in. I didn't know any middle-class black people when I was growing up; we were all poor. Now there are black doctors, lawyers, and businessmen and businesswomen. Although poverty still exists, there are many blacks who own beautiful, large homes, the kind of houses I helped my mother clean as a teenager.

Politics have changed, too. In 1997, the capitol city of Jackson elected its first black mayor. In addition, the racists who murdered innocent black activists in the 1960s were finally brought to justice more than thirty years later. In 1994, KKK member Byron De La Beckwith, who killed NAACP Field Secretary Medgar Evers, was tried and sentenced to life in prison, where he died. Imperial Wizard Sam Bowers was convicted in 1998 and sentenced to life for conspiracy to commit the murder of Vernon Dahmer, a slain civil rights activist.

Mississippi has come a long way since its violent and racist past, but there is still much to be done. It is still the poorest state in this

A man cooking in a wood stove inside his home in Pocahontas, Mississippi, in 1994. Photo by Marc-Yves Regis I.

A woman washing her face in a "wash pan" at her home in Pocahontas, Mississippi, in 1994. The house has no indoor plumbing or electricity. Photo by Marc-Yves Regis I.

country and at the bottom of the list in education, income, and housing. During my last visit in the summer of 2003, my husband, son, and I went on a driving tour in Jackson and saw many run-down shotgun houses in the city. One black woman we talked to said she had lived in the same house for thirty years. The house was unpainted and had limited plumbing and no central heat or air conditioning. She pays only 100 dollars a month for rent. It reminded me of the sharecropper shack we lived in more than thirty years ago.

Seeing those poor conditions made me think of sharecropper Fannie Lou Hamer. At the 1964 Democratic Convention, she addressed the crowd and asked, "I question America. Is this America? The land of the free and the home of the brave?" I, too, question America. How can the richest country in the world allow people to live in the same poverty that existed fifty years ago? I question America.

Acknowledgments

I would like to thank the civil rights movement's everyday heroes who fought outside the limelight to make this a peaceful, just, and humane world for all of God's children, no matter what race or color you are. I salute you.

Spirits flying all around
Superstition keeping us down
White folks changing like chameleons
Hanging black folks by the millions
Oh my God don't you hear us crying!
Oh my God don't you see us dying!

Stop the bloodshed! Stop this madness!
Bring us out of this evil darkness
Give us freedom; give us life
Deliver us from this iniquitous strife
Stop the white man. Stop the hoses!
Dethrone Pharaoh. Bring back Moses.
Bring us up North to the Promised Land.

Jim Crow memories living in my head
Mississippi ghosts sleeping in my bed
Jim Crow bosses at my job
Sabotaging my rise to the top

Acknowledgments

White folks' minds need an evolution
Black folks talking about a revolution
Evolution, revolution, evolution, revolution.
Neither one is a simple solution.

Frankye Regis

Introduction

When I was growing up in the bowels of racism in rural, segregated Mississippi in the 1960s and 1970s, it was considered a closed society. Racist whites controlled the state and no one, not even the mighty federal government, could tell them how to treat "their colored folks." They made sure that we lived in the poorest areas, worked the most demeaning jobs, and attended the worst schools.

Up until the mid-1960s, whites legally kept blacks from voting at city halls, riding city buses, playing at city parks, and swimming at city pools. Blacks couldn't even go to a public library. I do not remember ever going to a public library in Mississippi. In Jackson, there was the George Washington Carver Library, which was for blacks only, but I never went there. We lived in rural Mississippi, Mama couldn't drive, and Daddy worked two jobs and had no time to take us. Carver Library was segregated until 1975.

If a black person went shopping in town and got thirsty, he or she had to drink from a separate water fountain for "colored folks." Public bathrooms were also separate for blacks and whites. Every aspect of Southern life was governed by segregation. If a black person walked past a white person on the street, the black person dared not look the white person squarely in the eyes. It was a sign of disrespect for the master. A slave is not equal to his or her master. Slavery ended in 1865, but it seemed that no one had read the Emancipation Proclamation to the state of Mississippi and even parts of Alabama, Georgia, and Tennessee.

Introduction

After almost 300 years of slavery, blacks thought they finally had a chance to share in the fruits of their labor and be recognized as full-fledged citizens under the law. For a brief period during Reconstruction, blacks held political positions, owned land, and started businesses. This lasted for a few years until the KKK began terrorizing the black community. By the early 1900s, blacks were banned from public facilities and "kept in their place." Laws were implemented to institutionalize racism in every facet of Southern life. Whites enjoyed all the privileges life had to offer, and they did it all in the name of God. Most of the Klan were God-fearing people who ruled the South with a Bible in one hand and a rope and burning cross in the other.

But after a while, blacks grew tired. They were tired of the abuse. Tired of the oppression. Tired of being second-class citizens. After tiring of the slow progress that nonviolent protest brought, blacks latched on to the Black Power movement. No longer were we willing to allow whites to decide our future. We wanted our freedom now. We wanted to live wherever we wanted, go to whatever school we desired, and get well-paying jobs. We wanted to be treated as full-fledged citizens of the United States of America, just as the Constitution guarantees. As Martin Luther King told us, we wanted to be able to shout, "Free at last, free at last, thank God Almighty, we're free at last."

Timeline

1619	Africans are first brought to America as indentured servants.
1857	Dred Scott, a slave, tries to free himself from his master in Wisconsin, a free territory at the time. The Supreme Court rules that black people are not citizens but property.
1862 September	President Lincoln issues the Emancipation Proclamation (effective January 1, 1863), which frees the slaves in all territories except those at war with the Union.
1866	The Civil War officially ends and the reconstruction of the South begins.
1883	The Supreme Court rules that the Civil Rights Act of 1875, which banned discrimination in public places, is unconstitutional.
1890	The state of Mississippi adopts a new constitution that requires voters to be able to read and understand it, or to interpret sections read to them.
1896	The Supreme Court in *Plessy v. Ferguson* rules that states have the right to provide

"separate but equal" facilities for black and white people.

1909   The National Association for the Advancement of Colored People (NAACP) is organized to fight for the civil rights of black people.

1911   The National Urban League is formed to help black people from the rural South adjust to city life in the North.

1940s   Mississippi bans integrated travel in taxicabs, unless the black person is the white person's servant.

1942   The Congress of Racial Equality (CORE) is organized.

1948   Strom Thurmond (former South Carolina senator who died in 2003) runs for president on a platform of racial segregation.

1954
May 17   The Supreme Court, in *Brown v. Board of Education*, rules that segregation in educational facilities is unconstitutional.

July   White supremacy hate groups like the Citizens Council (or White Citizens Council) form in Indianola, Mississippi, in the Delta.

1955
August 28   Emmett Till, a fourteen-year-old black boy, is murdered and mutilated by two white men after allegedly whistling or saying "Bye baby" to a white woman.

November   The Interstate Commerce Commission bans segregation on interstate buses.

December 1   Rosa Parks, an Alabama seamstress, sits in the front of a Montgomery city bus in a seat just behind the section reserved for whites and is arrested for refusing to give up her seat to a white passenger. Black leaders boycott city buses for more than a year.

1956

January 11   Mississippi passes an ordinance requiring "common carriers of persons" to maintain separate public waiting rooms and restrooms for whites and blacks.

February   Autherine Lucy enrolls at the all-white University of Alabama under federal order.

December 21   The Montgomery bus boycott ends after a federal court rules that bus segregation is unconstitutional.

1957

January 11   The Atlanta-based Southern Christian Leadership Conference (SCLC) is established to help fight segregation.

August 30   Congress passes a civil rights act that strengthens blacks' voting rights. It also creates the Civil Rights Commission, which has the power to investigate voting abuses.

September   Nine black teenagers in Little Rock, Arkansas, are chosen to integrate Central High School after the school board designs a desegregation plan to comply with the *Brown* decision.

1958

May 29   One black student graduates from Central High School in Little Rock.

1959

May 5   Mack Charles Parker is lynched in Polarville, Mississippi.

1960

February 1   In Greensboro, North Carolina, four black college students sit down at a lunch counter reserved for whites only and refuse to leave. This direct challenge to segregation laws spurs sit-ins throughout the South.

Riots break out in New Orleans when four black girls go to first grade in an all-white school.

1961

January   James Meredith applies to enter the University of Mississippi.

March 27   The Tougaloo Nine (Mississippi high school students who are members of the Tougaloo NAACP Youth Council) go to the whites-only Jackson Municipal Public Library in Mississippi and refuse to leave. They are arrested and charged with breach of peace.

May 4   Freedom Rides, which are conducted to integrate interstate travel on buses, begin.

September 20   Mississippi Governor Ross Barnett stands at the entrance of the University of Mississippi and blocks James Meredith from entering.

September 30   President John F. Kennedy orders U.S. marshals to the state to prepare for Meredith's arrival.

1962   The Mississippi legislature institutionalizes segregation laws by passing two bills that keep the Jackson city bus line segregated.

1963

January 14   Alabama Governor George Wallace, a segregationist, is sworn into office.

May 28   Three Tougaloo College students walk through the back door of Woolworth's department store and sit down at the lunch counter. They are refused service and taunted and beaten by angry whites. After hours of abuse, police throw them in jail.

June 11   Governor George Wallace, with troopers on guard, stands in the doorway of a building at the University of Alabama at Tuscaloosa and blocks two black students from entering.

Mississippi civil rights leader Medgar Evers, thirty-seven, is murdered on his driveway in Jackson.

August 18   James Meredith graduates from the University of Mississippi.

August 28   Martin Luther King leads the March on Washington—a demonstration for jobs, voting rights, and freedom—and stands on the mall between the Washington Monument and the Lincoln Memorial.

September 15   A bomb explodes at the 16th Street Baptist Church in Birmingham, Alabama, the headquarters of the SCLC. Several people are injured and four young black girls are killed.

November 22   President Kennedy is assassinated in Dallas.

1964
June   Freedom Summer begins in Mississippi. Thousands of mostly white college students flood the state to conduct voter registration drives and to establish schools and community programs. It is designed to open up Mississippi to the rest of the country.

August 4   Three civil rights workers, James Chaney, twenty-one, Michael Schwerner, twenty-four, and Andrew Goodman, twenty, are found buried in an

	earthen dam on the private property of a KKK member. They have been missing since June 21.
August 27	The Mississippi Freedom Democratic Party sends a delegation to the national Democratic Convention in New Jersey and asks to represent the state officially on the convention floor.
December 10	Martin Luther King wins the Nobel Peace Prize.

1965

March 7	Demonstrators marching from Selma to Montgomery, Alabama, are savagely beaten by police when they reach the Edmund Pettus Bridge. This event comes to be known as "Bloody Sunday."
August 6	President Lyndon Johnson signs the Voting Rights Act into law.

1966

June	James Meredith, who integrated Ole Miss, leads the "March Against Fear," a 220-mile pilgrimage through Mississippi to encourage black people to register to vote. Meredith is shot but not seriously injured.

1968

April 4	James Earl Ray shoots and kills Martin Luther King as he stands on the balcony of the Lorraine Motel in Memphis, Tennessee. King was in Memphis to help city garbage collectors demonstrate for better working conditions. He was born in 1929.

Part I

The Roots of Racism and Oppression

Growing Up in Mississippi

I was born a second-class citizen.

The world I was born into was not promising. It was poor, backward, and segregated. Although my family rejoiced at my birth, the outside world didn't deem my life worthy. Because I was born black and female, I had a double whammy against me.

Growing up in Mississippi was a hard life. I was born in a sharecropper's shack in the backwoods of Mississippi. It was a densely wooded area we called "The Pines" on the outskirts of Jackson, about fifteen miles north of the city limits on Highway 49. Daddy paid a white man about two and a half dollars a month for us to live in that old shack on his sprawling land. In rural Mississippi, we were isolated from the world, an unjust, violent, segregated, and racist world.

All but the two youngest of my mother's eight children were born at home. Mama was pregnant fourteen times, but only eight survived. I was number six. Working in the cotton fields took a toll on her fragile and sickly body, and six babies were either stillborn or miscarriages. Mama was born with asthma and many times she was too sick to go to the clinic in nearby Clinton to see one of the few white doctors who treated blacks. Daddy would send word to the doctor, who would come to our house and give Mama oxygen to help her breathe. There were no hospitals close by and even if there were, I don't think Daddy could afford to take Mama there.

A midwife delivered me. I came out kicking and screaming at 5 P.M. on a muggy Sunday in April. Mama said I screamed every weekend thereafter for months. I like to think I cried so much because in some odd way, I knew the kind of world I had entered.

That year, a man named Mack Charles Parker was lynched in Polarville, Mississippi. As was always the case in the Deep South when

Mama and Daddy in the late 1980s. Author's original family photograph.

there was a lynching, he had been accused of raping a white woman. But two days before his trial, a white mob took him from jail, murdered him, and threw his body in the Pearl River. The case went to the grand jury, but it refused to acknowledge that a lynching had taken place. This was typical Mississippi justice—white men commit murder and no one pays the price. This type of warped thinking resulted in thousands of blacks being lynched in the South.

Mama and Daddy never told me that story. I read about it in a book. Blacks were afraid to talk about lynching; it was as if they thought the walls had ears. I didn't learn about the lynchings that took place around me until I was in seventh grade, when an outspoken black English teacher told our homeroom class about the South's big dirty secret.

Daddy moved his family from shack to shack until he had a house built for us on land his father had left him and his six brothers and sisters. Daddy was a veteran who had served in World War II. He had been drafted into the Army and when he got out, he later volunteered for the Navy. So, he qualified for a low-interest, veteran's home loan.

The unpainted three-room shack we moved from had two bedrooms—one for Mama and Daddy and one for the children—and a kitchen. There was no electricity, no indoor plumbing, and no running water. At night we burned coal-oil lamps. Mama papered the walls with newspaper. There was a fireplace in Mama and Daddy's bedroom and we would all stand or sit close to the fire to keep warm. Sometimes the licking blaze seared the thin hair on our legs. One time a visitor stood so close to the fireplace that the intensity of the heat scorched her dress. The shack wasn't insulated. The cracks in the house were so large that Mama used to stuff rags in them to keep out biting wind during the winter. During the rainy season in the spring, Daddy put buckets throughout the house to catch dripping rain from the leaky tin roof.

The new house was much bigger and it was painted a dull orange. When we moved into the new house in November 1961, I cried and cried to go back home to the old shack. I was almost three years old. Mama gave birth to my brother Paul in January 1962. We had six rooms: a bedroom for Mama and Daddy; a bedroom for my four brothers who paired up in two bunk beds; a bedroom for me and my sisters, who slept together in a queen-sized bed; a dining room; a kitchen; and a living room. We had electricity but no running water. Between the living and dining rooms was an orange swinging door, like the ones you see in saloons in westerns. The house had a small front porch and a large oak tree in the front yard. There was a cherry tree in the backyard. Nearby was an outhouse. Because we had no indoor bathroom, Mama put a slop jar in each bedroom for us to pee in, especially at night.

When the cherries on the cherry tree ripened, my siblings and I would squash them and put them in jars. We added water and sugar, hoping our concoction would ferment into a homemade brew. There were peach and pear trees in an orchard in the pasture that ran alongside our house, surrounded by blackberry bushes and plum trees. When we went to pick peaches and pears for Mama to make preserves, she gave us empty molasses buckets to put the fruit in.

We also picked blackberries to make pies and plums to make jelly. We ate more plums than we brought home. We liked to shake salt on them; we shook salt on all our fruit. That's how we liked it and it was the only way we would eat it. We also laced raw vegetables, such as cucumbers, tomatoes, and celery, with salt.

We got our water from a cistern that a family friend, Mr. Charlie Bass, Daddy, and my oldest brothers built. They dug a big hole in the ground on the side of the house not far from the kitchen and the backyard. I remember their mixing cement and pouring it into that big hole. They plastered the bottom and sides of the hole with wet cement and my brothers used sticks to write their names in it before the cement hardened. Mr. Charlie Bass wrote the year—1962. Then they hung gutters along the edge of the roof and down into the cistern so rainwater would drain directly into it.

I don't remember how deep the cistern was, but we were forbidden from playing around it. If it rained a lot, the cistern was full and we didn't have to drop the bucket far down to draw water. If there was a drought, which occasionally occurred, we let the entire rope down into the cistern, stood on our tiptoes, and leaned over to get a full bucket of water. Sometimes when we lowered the bucket and rope into the cistern and drew it out, bugs, crickets, or other insects floated on top. We just flicked them off and toted the water into the house.

We drew water for drinking, cooking, and bathing. At bath time, Mama would boil water in a pot on the stove. We had two types of aluminum tubs—a small, round one for the children and a long, oval-shaped one for the grown-ups. Baths were taken in birth order, starting with the oldest. Mama didn't throw out the water after each bath; she just added a fresh pot of hot water to the tub. When we were young, Mama would put two or three children at once in the big tub to save time.

The cistern was the first place visitors stopped on a sizzling summer day. Mama placed the draw bucket upside down on top of the cistern. Some people had aluminum dippers hanging on the side of their cisterns for passersby who wanted a cool drink, but Mama said that wasn't sanitary and she instead gave water in glasses. Sometimes whites traveling in their cars would stop by, go to blacks' cisterns, and take a drink out of their dipper or bucket without asking. Mama did not like that.

We spent most of our young lives going to church all day on Sundays, going to school on weekdays, and working in the fields after school and on Saturdays. Daddy was a farmer and he used every inch of his land to grow something. His big money-making crop was cotton. Back then, cotton was a major form of income for Mississippi, which was known as the "King of Cotton." Daddy sometimes kept us out of school if there was a big crop of cotton to pick in the fall.

During the summer months when school was out, Daddy got us up at 6 A.M. to work in the field. We worked in the field from sunup to sundown. The temperature hovered somewhere between 100 and 120 degrees by mid-day. We wore long-sleeve shirts, long pants, and straw hats to protect our bodies from the unrelenting sun. Each of us had a hoe according to our size. My brothers sharpened them with files each morning before we headed out to the field.

We walked along the dirt road that ran beside the orange house to "the bottom" across the creek. Weeds fanned out of deep ditches on either side of the narrow road. If Mama wasn't with us, we kicked at the dust and rocks that were embedded in the dirt with our steel-toed brogans.

If there was honeysuckle in the ditch, we pulled up a bunch, broke the flowers off the stems, and sucked out the juice. At the

A Mississippi cotton field. Photo by Marc-Yves Regis I.

Daddy in 1999 still plowing. Photo by Marc-Yves Regis I.

creek, we sat on the edge of the bridge and watched the fish swim around. When the creek was shallow, my brothers walked down into it and tried catching one of the few fish stuck in the mud, or they threw rocks at frogs.

My brothers usually brought along a shotgun to kill snakes that happened upon us in the field. The gun had a powerful kick, and the force would knock my brothers backward when they fired it. Sometimes we saw cottonmouths, rattlesnakes, and black snakes.

When the price of cotton dipped, Daddy planted other crops to supplement his income. He planted gardens that were as large as his cotton crops and the work was just as hard. Some vegetables were grown from seeds and some were plants that had to be set in the soil. Sometimes Daddy hired a white man from Pocahontas, Mississippi, to cultivate the land with a tractor. We liked to brag that Daddy had a white man working for him. After years of blacks working in whites' fields, we saw this as some sort of justice, or more so a status symbol for Daddy.

Plowing was man's work, but the girls still had to help with the planting. Planting seeds was easy. We dug holes in the mound of dirt on each row, threw the seeds in, and covered them with dirt. The worst job for me was setting plants. Daddy bought bundles of sweet potato plants and kept them moist until we planted them. We bent over on our hands and knees and used our fingers to push the plants into the soft, crumbly soil. I hated getting dirt underneath my fingernails.

In the fall, my brothers plowed up the sweet potatoes and we walked along the rows picking them up and putting them into small burlap sacks. We carried the sacks to a small garden near our house, dumped the potatoes in a pile on the ground, and covered them with a big stack of hay. We ate sweet potatoes all winter. Mama made candied yams and sweet potatoe pies or she baked the potatoes in the oven.

The work never ended. After picking and storing the potatoes for the winter, Daddy had us dig up peanuts, another dirty job because they grew underground. He didn't plant peanuts often and I was glad. When we pulled them up, we shook clumps of dirt off the vine and hung the peanuts up to dry. All of our hard work paid off when we roasted them in the oven and juggled them in our hands because they were too hot to eat.

One year, cucumbers were a hot item for farmers and Daddy planted acres of them. Every other day we had to pick them because they reproduced quickly. There were also beans, okra, and tomatoes to pick. We had to shuck corn and peel sugar cane, shell peas and snap beans. If Daddy saw us relaxing, he would find something for us to do. "An idle mind is the devil's workshop," he used to say.

Mama visiting Milwaukee in 1970. Author's original family photograph.

If blacks were second-class citizens in Mississippi, then black women were at the very bottom of Southern society. Women and girls did all of the cooking and cleaning. In our family, my brothers worked in the fields all day, but when it was time to chop or pick cotton, everybody went to the field. But the women still had to do the cooking and all the housework. The men did nothing in the house, from Daddy down to my brothers. Daddy said that housework was woman's work, but when it came to working in the fields, he had a double standard.

Mama usually cooked three meals a day. Most of the food she prepared was fried—fried pork sausages and chops, fried chicken, fried potatoes, fried bacon, fried corn, and fried green tomatoes. There was bread at every meal. Biscuits to sop molasses at breakfast, white bread at lunch, and cornbread at dinner.

Before Daddy bought Mama a wringer washing machine, Mama washed clothes outside underneath the "Big Tree," an oak. She drew water from the cistern and dumped it into the long aluminum tub we bathed in at night. She had another tub for rinsing the clothes. I used to watch Mama put a washboard into the soapy water and scrub the clothes with lye soap that Daddy made from pig fat after he killed a hog. She did this every day. Her knuckles would be raw from continuously rubbing clothes on that rough-edged board for hours. After rinsing the clothes, Mama hung them on clotheslines in the backyard. By the time Mama taught me to wash, we had an automatic washing machine, but I still had to hang clothes outside.

It was hard because Mama was picky about how she wanted me to hang them on the clothesline. Pants and shirts had to be hung a certain way. If I hung them up wrong, Mama would make me take them down and hang them the way she liked. She said it was embarrassing, the way I hung them. I thought this was ludicrous. Who cared how our clothes looked on the clothesline? Mama did though, and she assumed everyone else did too.

We worked so hard that we didn't have time to think much about our segregated life in Mississippi. Living out in the sticks kept us protected from the violence that raged in Jackson and throughout the state. Mama and Daddy didn't talk much about it. They feared for their lives like most other blacks. No one talked about Jim Crow

Mama sitting in her living room on Mother's Day, May 9, 1976. Author's original family photograph.

laws or segregated public facilities. They accepted it as a way of life. That was the way things had been all their lives, and as far as they were concerned, things would remain that way. Mississippi made sure of that back in 1962 when the state legislature institutionalized Jim Crow laws by passing two bills that kept the Jackson city bus line segregated. These were in addition to the ordinances that officials had passed at city hall in the 1940s, which banned integrated travel in taxicabs unless the black person was the white person's servant. In 1956, officials passed an ordinance requiring "common carriers of persons" to maintain separate waiting rooms and restrooms for whites and blacks.

Blacks in rural Mississippi didn't have access to local transportation service. My oldest brother Jerry said the Greyhound bus line that ran along Old Highway 49 allowed blacks to ride the bus in segregated seating. Jerry said he sometimes rode the bus to town with Daddy. They would walk down to the highway, which was about one mile from our home, and stand beside the road waiting for the bus. Daddy paid a quarter and my brother rode for free until he was five. They had to sit in the back of the bus.

Jerry said there was another bus for blacks, "Payne's Bus," which was owned by a black man. Blacks would stand beside the road and

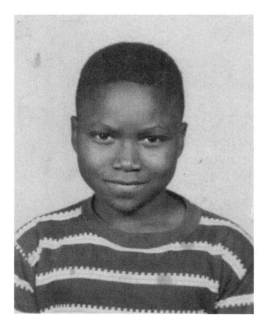

**Frankye's brother Jerry at school in 1962.
Author's original family photograph.**

wave a handkerchief as the bus approached. They could sit where they pleased on Payne's Bus. The fare was 25 cents for adults and a dime for children. Payne's bus started at 6 A.M., passed the "Drapers Place" plantation on whose property Mama and Daddy lived, and proceeded down the highway to Jackson. Riders had to arrange in advance if they wanted the driver to detour and pick them up at a different place. Payne's Bus stopped at Farish Street, the bustling downtown shopping area for blacks. If people wanted to leave earlier than that, they caught a Greyhound bus, which went as far north as Chicago but made local stops along Highway 49.

As a child, I was happy living in a neighborhood with people who looked like me and cared about me. I knew no other way. I enjoyed going to an all-black school. Everyone knew each other and their families. White people lived all around us but we had no contact with them. We didn't need them. I don't recall ever having a conversation with a white person while I was growing up in Mississippi.

Personal relationships between blacks and whites were almost nonexistent. In public, racist whites called blacks "nigger" to their faces. They humiliated black men by calling them "boy," and for some blacks, the degradation stripped them of their self-esteem. In private, blacks referred to whites as "crackers," "rednecks," and "peckerwoods." Political correctness was a thing for the future. Mississippi was a white man's world. The only time a black person was allowed to enter the white world was to spend money in their stores or to work in their homes.

Whites with old money lived in big, beautiful antebellum or colonial-style homes. The only time blacks set foot inside those houses was to clean them or cook for the owners. My grandmother, Granny, used to work for a white woman named Mrs. England who had a British accent. My brother Jerry said that the white woman was a lawyer and Granny was a nanny to her children. She lived in a large white house with columns that appeared to touch the roof. Granny also used to help out her friend who worked for a white woman named Mrs. Turner. Granny's friend served food at the lavish dinner parties the woman hosted.

Not all white people in Mississippi were prosperous. There were many who were as poor as black people. Everyone called them "poor white trash." I have no idea why. Regardless of their circumstances,

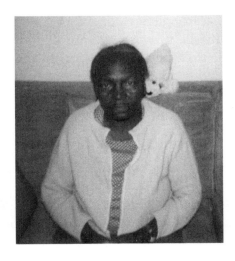

Granny sitting in Frankye's family's living room in the mid-1970s. Author's original family photograph.

some of them considered themselves better than black people and were more brutal toward us. I think that some rich whites who didn't want to get their hands dirty got the poor whites to do their dirty work of beating and lynching blacks.

Prominent whites organized private groups to stir up fear and dissent by proclaiming that integration would taint their closed society. They urged whites to fight against sending their children to the same schools as black children, living side by side in equal housing, and eating at the same restaurants with blacks. And, God-forbid, marrying their women. That was the cardinal sin for white men—the fear that black men would marry their women, or worse, rape them on sight. White women were put on a pedestal for the world to see, but for the black man not to touch. White women were forbidden fruit.

On the flip side, white men had their way with black women and there was nothing the women could do about it. In Mississippi I went to school and church with blacks with fair skin and blue or green eyes. I thought they were white until Mama said the children were the result of white men forcing the black women who worked for them into sexual liaisons. Sometimes it was the employers' sons who fathered illegitimate children. The white power structure turned its ugly head and didn't force these deadbeat dads to take care of their children. The women kept their mouths shut if they wanted to keep their jobs.

Take the case of long-time South Carolina Senator Strom Thurmond, who died in 2003. In 1948, when he was governor of that state, he ran for president on a platform of racial segregation. But as a twenty-two year old he had fathered a child with a sixteen-year-old black girl who worked as a domestic in his family's home. His illegitimate black daughter, who is in her mid-70s, spoke on the television news show *60 Minutes* shortly after Thurmond's death about her father who she said took care of her financially in secret. Not all of these illegitimate children were so lucky.

Sometimes the white women fought back, but their wrath was always against the black women because white women, too, were oppressed by white men. Granny often told a story about a black woman who worked for a young white family in Jackson. The woman became pregnant and had a baby who looked white. When the white man's wife heard rumors that the baby was her husband's, she went to the black woman and told her to leave Mississippi or else. The black woman took no chances and left the state for good.

It was easy for the white men to hide their double lives. In the 1950s and 1960s, the majority of domestic workers were black women. Not many black people had cars back then and even white families usually had only one car. In some cases, white men picked up black women for work and dropped them off late in the evening, so it was not unusual for them to be alone together in a car. While growing up, I constantly heard rumors about mixed couples making out in cars parked along pitch-black country roads. But a black man would be mutilated and hung on a tree if he was caught alone with a white woman. White men were afraid that black men would do to white women what they were doing to black women. White women were white men's property and black women were considered lower than that. There was no love; it was all about power and sex. Black women were invisible.

To the outside world—the white world—I was invisible. No one asked about my hopes and dreams, and no one cared. All they saw was a poor black girl who was destined to become an unwed teenage mother drowning in poverty and misery. If they had asked me what I wanted to be when I grow up, I would have told them an artist, a writer, a poet. Instead, they created a wall of stereotypes that blinded their perceptions of me. They never got to know me; they never saw me.

I had big dreams, but Mama, Daddy, and that cotton field were killing them. I longed to be a painter. I wanted to leave the South and travel all over the world. At an early age, I discovered that I could draw well and I thought my art would be my ticket out of Mississippi.

When I was about twelve, I told Daddy I wanted to drop out of regular school and go to art school. I loved to draw. I was drawing before I was walking. In school, my teachers asked me to draw and color pictures to display on their classroom walls. At home, I found discarded boards and drew pictures on them. I once drew a picture from my Bible of Jesus praying in the garden of Gethsemane before

He was crucified. I didn't have oils or acrylics to paint with, so I colored it with my crayons. I was taught to pray to God when I had a problem. It was hard for me to pray to a God I couldn't see, so I prayed for Him to reveal Himself to me. I never saw God, but my Sunday school teacher told us that Jesus and God were one spiritual being. It took me a long time to understand that revelation. I didn't look at the picture when I prayed at night though. I knew better than to pray to an idol, but I felt safer with the picture of Jesus hanging on the wall, seemingly watching over me. Mama kept that picture for years. The colors faded, but Jesus' face was still visible.

I was always looking for something interesting to draw. I enjoyed looking through magazines that Mama brought home from the houses of white people where she worked part-time while we were at school. She started working after Robert, the youngest child in our family, started first grade. The magazines had entry forms for drawing contests and I won each one I entered. One of the contest's officials sent a representative, a tall, heavy, dark-haired white man, to our house to talk to Mama and Daddy about my taking courses at an art school up North somewhere. Daddy said no.

Looking back, the contests were probably scams to take people's money, especially innocent black people who knew better than to accuse a white man of cheating them. But I can't remember if Daddy said no because he couldn't afford the classes or because I was too young. When Daddy said no to something, he never explained why, so maybe I never knew the reason. I was devastated. I had read about the French painters Pierre Renoir and Claude Monet and made up my mind that I must live in France to be as good as those guys. I dreamed of living in Paris and drinking fine wine like a good artist should. When Daddy said no, I vowed never to draw again. I was too depressed to motivate myself to draw, and there wasn't anyone else around to lift my spirits. Everyone had their own crosses to bear. I tried talking to Granny, my best friend at the time, about my problem. Although she was sympathetic, she didn't quite understand my need for freedom to pursue my dream of becoming an artist. Eventually the dream died. (I took some art classes in college and then again later in life, but the feelings I had about art as a child were never the same.)

I started writing poetry to relieve my hurt. One day, some friends at school looked over my shoulder and watched while I wrote poems in class. A girl snatched one of the poems out of my notebook and showed it to the English teacher. She asked me to read it aloud to the class and a writer was born. I can't recall the name of the poem. All I remember is that it was about some poor little oppressed black girl. I kept a notebook of my poetry and all my school papers under my bed, but during one of Mama's annual spring-cleaning sprees, she called me a pack rat and threw out all of my stuff. I never saved any of my beloved writings at home again.

Because the outside world didn't see me, no one else did either, not even my parents. It was not easy growing up in a large family. There were too many children for Mama and Daddy to give each one individual attention. Most of the time, they forgot I was alive. I was quiet in a house that was lively and boisterous. I never liked talking much. Didn't have much to say. There wasn't much that interested me. Therefore, everyone forgot about me most of the time. I preferred to curl up with a good book and read in my room. When I came out, I would sometimes see two of my brothers, the youngest of our brood, licking lollipops or munching cookies or whatever treats Mama and Daddy had brought home that day. I asked for mine and Mama would say, "We forgot about you, you're always so quiet and never come out of your room."

I learned to do without at an early age. I asked Mama and Daddy for nothing and I got nothing. Of course they provided for my basic needs, but I never begged for anything extra. Why would I frustrate myself by asking for things I knew I couldn't get? I gladly accepted the hand-me-down clothes that people gave us because I knew my parents couldn't afford anything else. I couldn't wear much of my older sisters' clothes because of the different sizes. I am the tallest girl in the family. When school started, though, I usually got a new pair of shoes and two new outfits. The clothes never fit properly because Mama bought them two sizes too big so I could grow into them. This wasn't a problem for me in elementary school because I wore dresses most of the time and I was lanky with long legs. My legs were longer than my body, so the dresses didn't sag because of my height.

Mama and Frankye in 1980. Author's original family photograph.

Junior high school was a different story. At the time, blue jeans and T-shirts were the popular school dress. The girls usually wore tight jeans to show off their figures. Some kids at school laughed at me because my pants were always too big. My feelings were hurt, but I didn't let them show. I didn't tell Mama because I knew she couldn't do anything. She had more important things to worry about and there was nothing else for me to wear. I tried taking up the slack in my pants by sewing the seams together but I was never good at domestic tasks and the pants bunched up and shortened. They looked awful. I don't know if I was too embarrassed to tell anyone or if anyone really cared. I kept it to myself. Eventually clothes just didn't matter to me. After a while, nothing really mattered anymore. I wanted to be a free spirit, left alone to do my own thing.

Black pride was still going strong in the seventies and radio stations were playing James Brown's "Say it Loud, I'm Black and I'm Proud." I wore my hair in braids or an Afro. I liked the natural look. Mama would insist that I not leave the house unless my hair was acceptable. An invisible child has no voice. I was disenfranchised. I took things as they came and tried my best to survive. I couldn't wait to become an adult. Individuality had no place in rural Mississippi. You either conformed or everyone around you tried to break your spirit. Everything was about race, or more specifically, skin tone.

In school, children use to parrot this rhyme: "If you're white, you're right; if you're brown, stick around; if you're black, get back." I don't know who coined this phrase, but black children clearly understood what it meant—blacks were considered inferior to everyone else on the face of the earth. We knew that whites wanted us in the back—in the backs of buses and trains and the last in everything that society offered. We knew that our schools, our books, and our homes were unequal. The sad part is that children at my school compared skin tones and said this rhyme to their own peers. Mississippi's racist white society had done exactly what it intended—divided us to keep us oppressed.

During slavery, light-skin blacks were chosen to work in their masters' homes on cotton plantations. Sometimes they were children that the master had fathered with a black slave. President Thomas Jefferson allegedly fathered children with one of his black slaves, Sally Henning, and they worked in his house.

These actions caused resentment among dark-skin blacks, who worked in the cotton fields under poor conditions. The light-skin blacks were called "house niggas," and the dark-skin blacks were called "field niggas." Blacks who worked in the mansions were treated better. They got to wear nicer clothes and could eat the whites' leftovers. The skin-tone rivalry continued well after slavery ended. The lighter your skin, the more opportunities you had.

In the 1960s, when blacks demanded better jobs and pay, the few blacks that whites did hire to work in their stores and shops were blacks with fair skin. It wasn't that whites accepted light-skin blacks as equals. Even if a black person could pass for white, whites still considered him or her black. There was a rule in the South that a person with one drop of black blood was black, no matter what physical characteristics he or she had. If the federal government was going to force whites to integrate, then they could only tolerate being around blacks who looked like them. This thinking seeped into the black community and caused deeper divisions between light and dark-skin blacks.

Dark-skin blacks felt that some light-skin blacks considered themselves superior to their own race, even if that was not the case. A light-skin black person who married someone with darker skin usually had children with varying skin tones. Divisions were also created within families if one of the parents or grandparents gave preferential treatment to the light-skin children. They knew their fair-skin children would be more accepted in the white world. The comparison scarred some blacks for life.

There were cases where blacks were so fair that they could pass for white, and some did. Their skin color was their ticket out of poverty and they gained acceptance in a world of white privilege. In New Orleans, some mixed-raced people, known as Creoles, formed organizations and instructed members to marry only people who looked like them under the guise of preserving their so-called multicultural race.

Discrimination against dark-skin blacks found its way into some Southern black colleges. There was an unwritten policy called the "brown paper bag test" where only blacks whose skin color was lighter than a paper bag would be admitted. I used to wonder why some of the educated and articulate black leaders I saw on television looked white. For example, Thurgood Marshall, the late Supreme Court Justice, had fair skin and fine hair. New York Congressman Adam Clayton Powell could also pass.

To some whites in the South, black was synonymous with ugly; they called us "baboons" and "coons" and any other derogatory names they could think of to put us down and make themselves feel better. They compared us with animals and portrayed us as savages when they were the ones carrying out the brutality. Their intent was to destroy our self-esteem and our spirits.

At school, when we wanted to hurt each other's feelings, we used the same hurtful names that whites called us. The ultimate insult was to call someone a "dog," but a "black dog" drew a severe pun-ishment, a beating from our parents or, at school, being sent to the principal's office. Back then, "black" was considered a bad thing to call someone. By design or otherwise, the racist white system of showing color preference was successful in getting an oppressed people to take on the views of their oppressors. Even the light-skin blacks who were the product of a black parent and a Native Ameri-can bragged about having white blood. No one wanted to be black, not even blacks.

All I know is I didn't feel inferior to whites. I loved the color of my skin. I felt there was nothing I couldn't do. I had everything fig-ured out. I was going to keep reading and educating myself, and I was going to get a scholastic scholarship and leave Mississippi behind.

Early African-American History

Some blacks now take it for granted that they can live where they want to, send their children to whatever schools they please, choose to eat in any restaurant they like, and use public facilities. They have known no other way.

However, only forty years ago this was not the case, especially in the Deep South. Blacks were beaten, jailed, or murdered just for fighting for freedom, justice, and the right to be treated as human beings, which is guaranteed in the U.S. Constitution.

However, the fight for civil rights didn't begin in the 1960s; it began in the 1800s when slavery was still prevalent in the South. When blacks were first brought to the British American colonies at Jamestown, Virginia, in 1619, they were considered indentured servants. While indentured servants from other countries were freed after completing their service, over time, laws were created that permitted owners to keep Africans as slaves. Africans were bound with chains and forced to this country in crowded ships to work in unbearable heat on white people's farms. Although blacks fought for America's independence in the Revolutionary War, they were not granted freedom in the 1770s, when the Constitution was written. Slavery was not addressed in the Constitution because the founding fathers knew that the Southern states would not be a part of the union if slavery were banned.

I have wrestled with this reasoning most of my adult life. How could a country that proclaims freedom and liberty for all allow a privileged group of people to enslave another group of people for almost 250 years? I also ask myself why blacks allowed these people to enslave, brutalize, and oppress them for all those years? Why weren't they militant, like the people of Haiti who defeated the French in 1804 and gained their independence? Haiti paid a heavy political price for its militancy and was isolated by other countries, especially countries that had slaves. The United States refused to recognize the black island country in the Caribbean because they thought that blacks in this country would get the same idea.

I remember the fear of the old black people in Mississippi who were afraid to look a white person in the eyes. They feared being beaten or killed for speaking their minds or for standing up for their human rights.

I think how it must have felt to be kidnapped from your family and home and forcibly brought to a country in chains thousands of miles away. What state of mind were the slaves in when they arrived, after so many died because of hunger, thirst, and disease on filthy ships? How did it feel not knowing the language, customs, or people? How did it feel to be brutalized and beaten and forced to work in tobacco, sugar cane, and cotton fields all day long without pay? Then they had to come home to slave quarters and eat milk-and-bread (cornbread and sugar soaked with butter milk) and sleep in crowded shacks. If a slave was brave enough to attempt to run away, he or she was beaten into oblivion as an example to others.

The oppression and brutality of slave owners were so great that the fear that blacks had of whites was still around when I was growing up in Mississippi. It was then that I understood that there had been no way out for blacks. Racism and discrimination were rooted into the psyche of the Southern white political structure.

The founding fathers did not include slaves in the Bill of Rights. Slaves did not even have legal protection over their children. They were the master's property. Slaves were sold or traded at will. After the Revolutionary War, free black people couldn't vote, serve on a jury in any state, or serve in the military.

Not everyone believed that slavery was right. The Abolitionist Movement was in full swing in the 1830s. Before the Civil War, abolitionists set up a system to help runaway slaves escape to free states or to Canada. Former slave Sojourner Truth was an abolitionist and so was Harriet Tubman, who was also called Moses after the biblical prophet who led the Israelites out of slavery in Egypt to the Promised Land. Although she was badly beaten by a slave owner and had blackouts because of it, she led hundreds of slaves to freedom by moving them from house to house under the cover of darkness. Frederick Douglass, a former slave, was one of the movement's leaders. He spoke out against segregated seats on trains and he used his home as a stop on the Underground Railroad. He also discussed slavery issues with President Lincoln.

In 1857, Dred Scott, a slave, tried to free himself from his master because they lived in Wisconsin, which was then a free territory. The U.S. Supreme Court ruled that blacks were not citizens; they were property and Congress had no power to take away whites' property by banning slavery in the territories.

When it came to taxation and representation, the U.S. Constitution said that Negro slaves were only three-fifths of a person. The Confederate States of America used that declaration to support their cause. Some Southern states decided to secede from the union because they wanted to maintain slave labor in their fields. Abraham Lincoln, who was president at the time, led the nation into a Civil War to preserve the union. For years we were taught in school that Lincoln freed the slaves because he didn't like slavery. That is not true. In fact, states that supported the union could keep their slaves. Lincoln's decision to free some of the slaves was purely a political move to convince Confederate states to stop fighting.

In 1862 Lincoln delivered the Emancipation Proclamation, which took effect on January 1, 1863. It freed all slaves except those who lived in states that did not rebel against the national government. Lincoln also allowed blacks to serve in the military in segregated units. The U.S. Colored Troops helped recruit other black soldiers who served as nurses, laborers, and guides.

In 1866 the Civil War officially ended and the Reconstruction period began. Many of the large plantations were taken from rebel owners. Some land was given to free slaves, called "freedmen." Not only could freedmen own land, but their marriages were also recognized by law and they could start families. They were free to worship however they pleased and go wherever they pleased without permission from white people. Many left the plantations and looked for family members who had been sold or traded during slavery.

But without money, land, full legal protection, and the right to vote, blacks still struggled for their civil rights. Black leaders rose up and pushed for equal rights. The government promised each black family forty acres and a mule, but this promise was never brought to fruition. I remember Granny joking about still waiting for her forty acres and a mule, but as a child I had no idea what she was talking about. Who would want that? To me, it seemed like more work for blacks.

After the war, white Southerners created Black Codes to keep the races separate and under whites' control. Mixed marriages were illegal, blacks could not own a gun, and they had to work for whites. They could not testify in court against whites. Sharecropping replaced slavery as a way of life. Blacks were forced to plant and harvest whites' farms for half of the profit. But blacks always ended up in debt after each crop and seemed indebted to farm owners for life, since the only person willing to give them financial credit was the landlord, who charged exorbitant prices for seeds, equipment, and necessities.

The house that Daddy built for Granny. Daddy's little red store is next door. His family's orange house is nearby. Author's original family photograph.

In 1865 the Freedmen's Bureau was set up to help former slaves get their own land, and, with the help of Northern churches, public and private schools were created. Blacks made considerable progress during Reconstruction's ten-year period: Congress and the country passed the 13th Amendment, which officially ended slavery in all states; two years later, the 14th Amendment gave blacks citizenship rights and equal protection under the law, and the 15th Amendment gave them the right to vote. Because of that, blacks were elected and served in Congress and the Senate during Reconstruction.

Eventually Reconstruction failed and Congress closed the Freedmen's Bureau. The Northern states wanted to put the war behind them and allowed white Southerners to take complete control of the South.

Public schools for blacks were underfunded and more than half of the black population was illiterate. Blacks suffered unbearable racial discrimination and violence. It seemed that each time blacks gained a civil right, the Supreme Court took it away. In 1883, the Court ruled that the Civil Rights Act of 1875, which had banned discrimination in public places, was unconstitutional. As a form of intimidation, a white supremacist group called the Ku Klux Klan (KKK) burned crosses on blacks' lawns.

Blacks who violated the Black Codes were lynched. Former slaves who tried to open their own businesses were intimidated. The laws were intended to oppress, disenfranchise, and keep blacks in dire poverty. Anyone who dared to speak out for equal treatment was hanged on a tree and left there to send a message to other blacks who crossed the sacred white divide.

Racist white Southerners balked at extending equal treatment to blacks, who looked to the courts to enforce the law. The courts, however, sided with segregationists. In 1896, Homer Plessy, a black man from New Orleans, was arrested for riding in a railroad car reserved for whites. The Supreme Court, in *Plessy v. Ferguson*, ruled that states had the right to provide "separate but equal" facilities for blacks and whites, even though everyone knew these facilities were far from equal.

Blacks lived in extreme poverty. At the end of the nineteenth century, lynching by white mobs was the preferred method of death for any black person who dared to make a decent living in the South. Thousands of blacks were hanged, mutilated, and tortured, and the white supremacist groups who carried out the vicious acts were neither arrested nor punished. Oftentimes black prisoners were released to these mobs. Many photographs and documentaries exist in which the killers posed for pictures after committing such violent acts. Men dressed in white robes stand smiling as black bodies with ropes tied around their bloody necks dangle from trees. In some photographs, white children stand with their parents watching what appears to be entertainment for them.

Many prominent black leaders at the time spoke out against violence, injustice, and discrimination that blacks faced in the South. Ida B. Wells, a prominent black teacher and outspoken journalist, condemned the lynching of blacks. Born a slave during the Civil War, she attended a college sponsored by Northern missionaries during Reconstruction. She dismissed the explanation that whites lynched black men because they raped white women. She left Memphis after whites threatened to kill her for her openness. She forced a national debate on lynching and brought international attention to the subject.

Not all black leaders agreed on how to fight oppression. Booker T. Washington urged blacks to behave peacefully and get along with whites no matter what it took. Washington, founder of the Tuskegee Institute in Alabama, promoted education as a means for blacks to rise above their conditions. He was born in Virginia in 1856; his father was a white man. Washington was against blacks being involved in politics and seeking civil rights, suggesting that they work hard toward economic cooperation with whites.

Whites were against a broad education for blacks; they wanted them to learn trades, such as farming, sewing, and cooking so that they would be useful to white society and unable to make a decent living on their own. Whites were vehemently against paying taxes to fund public schools for black children, although blacks, too, paid taxes. Whites did not want an educated black society that could compete with them politically and financially. They wanted an uneducated black race that they could manipulate and oppress. But some blacks accused Washington of selling out his race because whites did not cooperate and the violence against blacks continued.

Washington and other black intellectuals continued to butt heads over the course of black education and what it would take to bring about equality. He considered the Reconstruction era, which gave blacks the right to vote and hold office, a mistake, while others highly praised its efforts. He believed blacks could gain independence through self-help, but that this could not happen if they focused too much on politics and failed to learn skills that would earn them a decent living.

Harvard graduate W.E.B. Du Bois encouraged blacks to fight for every right guaranteed them under the Constitution. Du Bois, born into freedom in the North in 1868, held a doctorate degree in history and published poems, novels, and several autobiographies. He grew up and attended school in Great Barrington, Massachusetts. He went to Fisk University in Nashville, and obtained a master's and doctorate from Harvard. His best known books are *The Souls of Black Folk* and *Up from Slavery*, an autobiography.

The National Association for the Advancement of Colored People (NAACP), which was formed in 1909 to fight for the rights of blacks as citizens, campaigned to end lynching. A group of well-educated and affluent blacks and whites founded the organization after a National Conference on the Negro was held in New York City. Du Bois was the director and editor of the organization's newspaper, *Crisis*.

James Weldon Johnson became the NAACP's field secretary in 1917. An Atlanta University graduate, Johnson was a lawyer who wrote poetry, founded a newspaper, published a novel, and served as a U.S. consul in Venezuela and Nicaragua. He was also the songwriter who wrote the Negro national anthem, "Lift Every Voice and Sing." In 1911, the National Urban League was formed to help blacks who had migrated from the rural South adjust to urban life in the North.

By the early 1900s, Southern blacks began leaving the South in droves, looking for a better life up North. Thus began the first wave of the Great Migration. While white men were off fighting in World War I, blacks took over factory jobs that paid much better than field labor. At the turn of the century, the majority of blacks still lived and worked in the South. Most worked in the fields and the ones in the city worked at low paying and unskilled jobs. In the South, black women worked mostly as domestics in whites' homes. In the North, however, they worked in public kitchens and laundries.

Meanwhile, President Wilson urged blacks to support America in the war effort. Black leaders protested. How could blacks wholeheartedly fight for the rights of people on another continent when they were subjected to racial segregation, violence, lynching, poor education, no voting rights, vagrancy laws, and oppression in their own country? Still, the U.S. government needed men to fight and the NAACP supported sending black men into the military. They were drafted in the Army and the NAACP pushed for some to be trained as officers at black-only camps. The black soldiers served in segregated units because the Army considered them inferior to whites. The Army unsuccessfully tried to get the French to practice segregation and discrimination of races when black soldiers were sent there. The Army asked French officers to segregate black troops to avoid angering white officers. But black troops were accepted socially by the French.

One of my great uncles (now deceased) said that when he served in the military in France, white officers told the French that black men were monkeys who grew tails at night. He said the lie was to keep white French women from dating black men. But the plan backfired because the women were curious to see the tails come out at night. My uncle used to let out a devious cackle when he recalled how the black men got many dates with women who were anxious to see them nude.

Black support of the war did nothing to change whites' attitudes. Jim Crow laws were increased to keep blacks in their place. Soldiers returning from the war rebelled and riots broke out in some cities in the South. White mobs in the North also viciously attacked and killed some blacks who had migrated to the North, accusing them of taking away their jobs.

Blacks counterattacked in a wave of black militancy. In 1919, black leader Marcus Garvey founded the Universal Improvement Association (UNIA) and urged blacks to reject white society. He had come to America from Jamaica in 1916 and joined black militancy groups in the North. Around this time, NAACP branches spread throughout the South. The group no longer consisted mainly of educated blacks; women and the poor also began joining the NAACP. Meanwhile, Garvey promoted black separatism and called for a back-to-Africa movement. Two years after he founded UNIA, the organization had grown faster than the NAACP and black women held key leadership roles in it. Garvey's first wife helped found the organization and his second wife helped edit the *Negro World,* the newspaper Garvey started.

Garvey also created the Black Star Line (BSL) Steamship Corporation and sold stock in the company. This was the only all-black ship that served blacks, who could now sail all over the Caribbean. BSL even set up trade agreements with Africa. But in 1922, Garvey's dream of liberation for Africa died. A federal grand jury indicted him and three other BSL officers on mail fraud charges. Financial problems forced the BSL to close. In 1923 Garvey was convicted and two years later he began serving a five-year sentence. After serving two years, the Federal Bureau of Investigation, led by J. Edgar Hoover, exiled Garvey to his homeland of Jamaica. Black leaders who did not agree with Garvey's segregationist views helped kick him out of America. Garvey later moved to London where he died. Within a few years, the mass movement of Black Nationalism had also died.

On a small scale, blacks continued fighting for their civil rights. In the 1930s, boycotts of white-owned stores in black communities resulted in a few jobs for blacks. The country was in a depression and people illegally rode freight trains in search of food and jobs. In 1931, four white boys jumped aboard a freight train in Alabama that was headed to Memphis. Four black boys were already on the train and five more came aboard. The black and white boys got into a fight and the black youth threw three of the white boys off the train. The white boys went to the nearest train station and reported the incident. They said the attack was unprovoked. Sheriffs' deputies searched the train at one of its stops and found the nine black boys still aboard. A white boy and two young white girls were also aboard. As the deputies were about to take the black youngsters to jail in Scottsboro, Alabama, the two white girls accused the black youth of raping them.

The case of the "Scottsboro Boys," who ranged in age from twelve to nineteen, went before an all-white male jury, which found eight of the nine guilty; they were sentenced to death in a trial that drew international attention to America's unjust judicial system and the plight of blacks. The judge declared the youngest boy's case a mistrial. The case was botched from the beginning because the doctors who examined the girls found no signs of rape. Also, the NAACP hesitated to represent the youths in court because the case was messy and the boys were illiterate and the organization felt they did not reflect the black race in a good light. However, when the International Labor Defense (ILD), which was controlled by the Communist Party, took over the case, NAACP officials fought with them, regarding the communists as crazy political opportunists. The ILD won the case on appeal in 1932 when the Supreme Court overturned the youth's convictions. The Court ruled that the defense was improperly handled, which in turn denied the young men a fair trial as granted in the 14th Amendment. A new trial was granted.

The ILD provided the chief defense attorney for the Scottsboro Boys when their new trial came up. The first defendant who was retried was found guilty by a jury that said he should be punished by death, but the judge set aside the conviction, saying the rapes did not take place. Alabama authorities were persistent; they tried the black man a third time, and they also set trials for the other seven with a new judge. The men were again found guilty of rape and faced the death penalty. The Supreme Court once again heard the case and the defendants' lawyer argued that the case was unconstitutional, successfully arguing that blacks were not chosen to serve on the jury solely because of their race. The Court agreed, saying that the defendants had faced racial discrimination.

Eventually, state prosecutors dropped charges against four of the black men but they retried the others, who received prison sentences ranging from twenty-five to ninety-nine years. One received a death sentence that was later commuted to life in prison. (By 1950, they were all released.)

Meanwhile, the Communist Party gained popularity among some blacks because it pushed self-determination, and it opposed economic oppression and racial segregation. The party did not believe in white supremacy and supported racial equality for all people. The party helped blacks in some Southern states form share-croppers' unions, and in 1935 it helped establish civil rights organizations like the National Negro Congress, a coalition that supported labor unions, churches, fraternal organizations, and civic groups. The party accepted blacks from all spectrums of life. International star Paul Robeson, who had starred in *Othello* on stage in London, sang "Ol' Man River" in *Showboat,* and starred in the movie *The Emperor Jones,* supported the Communist Party.

Still, with all its influence, the party did not create a mass movement for black liberation. In the South, blacks were severely punished for associating with communists, and in the North, the party failed to inspire a revolution. It was difficult for the party to represent a race of people that had vast and dangerous mountains to climb. Only black leaders could understand what was needed. In the 1930s, blacks took action into their own hands. In Harlem and Chicago, particularly, black nationalists organized sit-ins at white department stores that refused to hire them.

The other big problem blacks faced was the Great Depression itself. Franklin D. Roosevelt became president in 1933 and promised the people a "New Deal." Blacks, who had been overwhelming Republicans after the party was created during Reconstruction to push for equality, turned to the Democratic Party. Although both blacks and whites were starving and faced poverty, blacks were hit the hardest.

Black workers, who experienced discrimination from employers and white unions, formed their own unions. Black men serving mostly white passengers riding on the Pullman railroad cars formed the Brotherhood of Sleeping Car Porters union. A. Philip Randolph, a socialist and the editor of *The Messenger,* a magazine for blacks, was the chief organizer. The Pullman Company was against unions, but President Roosevelt supported them. In 1934, Congress passed the Railway Labor Act, which banned company unions and gave workers the right to organize as a group without backlash. In 1937, the Pullman Company was forced to sign a contract with Randolph's union and black workers got a pay increase and shorter working hours.

As Randolph's stature rose, the black unity movement returned. In 1936, at a convention in Chicago, multicultural delegates decided to form the National Negro Congress (NNC) and elected Randolph as its president. Randolph resigned a few years later because of disagreements over what he considered too much communist influence in the organization and because of the NNC's opposition to Roosevelt's New Deal, which eventually lifted the U.S. economy out of depression.

In 1941, Randolph threatened Roosevelt with a march on Washington of 100,000 people, with a demonstration at the Lincoln Memorial to protest unequal economic treatment of blacks and their lack of involvement in World War II. Whites were getting all of the federal defense contracts while blacks were excluded from the well-paying defense industry jobs in the North and South. Roosevelt pressured him to call off the march but Randolph refused unless the president did something to stop discrimination against blacks. The black community nationwide prepared to join the massive march.

Roosevelt blinked and issued an executive order that banned employment discrimination in defense and government industries. Randolph cancelled the march. (Although blacks served in World War II, they were still segregated and discriminated against. It wasn't until 1950–1953, during the Korean War, that American troops were integrated. The NAACP helped fuel these changes.)

In 1941, Congress created the Fair Employment Practices Committee but unions and employers resisted the committee until it had no teeth. Blacks were no better off than before. They still struggled for the right to vote and faced segregation in transportation, schools, housing, public accommodations, and the military.

Blacks continued to look for methods that would help them gain equality. Some black leaders became influenced by Gandhi and his nonviolent struggle that had gained India its independence from the British. In 1942, they created the Congress of Racial Equality (CORE) to implement nonviolent techniques. The group organized a sit-in at a Chicago restaurant to protest discrimination against blacks.

The NAACP took a different route from CORE. The group preferred to use the courts to challenge segregation. Baltimore native Thurgood Marshall, who had joined the organization in 1936 as an assistant, was now the principal legal strategist. In 1944, the Supreme Court in *Smith v. Allwright* banned the white primary, which had kept blacks from voting. With the NAACP's help, a Houston man had sued a state election official who refused to let him vote in the Democratic primary. The success of that suit inspired blacks to register to vote.

Black soldiers returning from World War II were now demanding the same rights that they had fought for others to have in Europe. In the South they still had to go through whites to do so and the threat of violence or death kept many from registering to vote. One of Daddy's brothers recalled a story about the time he returned to Mississippi from World War II and decided to exercise his right to vote as a U.S. citizen. The registrar's office was in the small town of Pocahontas, Mississippi. My uncle knew that white men beat blacks who attempted to register, so he thought about what he should do. He took notice of what time the men at the town office went to lunch and then he went to Town Hall and applied to register. In Mississippi, you had to own land to vote and he satisfied that rule because my grandfather owned several acres.

In 1890, Mississippi had adopted a new constitution that required voters to be able to read and understand it, and, if the constitution was read aloud, voters also had to interpret a section of it. My uncle interpreted parts of the Constitution with ease. He was allowed to register because he succeeded in outsmarting the same people who claimed blacks were dumb, inferior, and uneducated.

To keep the races segregated in the capitol city of Jackson, officials implemented laws. In the 1940s, city officials passed an ordinance that prohibited taxicabs from carrying blacks and whites together unless the black person was a servant. In 1956, an ordinance was passed that created separate waiting rooms and restrooms for the two races.

The Modern Civil Rights Movement

Having achieved court successes on voting rights, the NAACP decided to go after Jim Crow laws, which enforced segregation of the races, especially in unequal schools. In the South, many blacks had attended schools in donated shacks. In the 1950s, instead of allowing black children to attend better funded white schools, state governments began building separate schools for black children that hardly provided an equal education. The walls of school segregation began to crumble on May 17, 1954, when the Supreme Court, in *Brown v. Board of Education,* ruled that segregation in educational facilities called "separate but equal," was unconstitutional. Representing black parents in Virginia, South Carolina, Louisiana, Kansas, Delaware, and Washington, D.C., the NAACP filed a lawsuit asking that their children be admitted to white schools.

The white South resisted the *Brown* decision and segregationist Senators James Eastland and John Stennis and Representative John Bell Williams of Mississippi, and South Carolina Senator Strom Thurmond tried to reverse the groundbreaking *Brown* decision. In addition, white supremacist resistance groups, such as the Citizens Council (or White Citizens Councils), formed in 1954 in Indianola, Mississippi, in the Delta also fought the decision. Members of these elite groups of segregationists were professionals and politicians.

Despite the rise in terrorism against blacks, they had a newfound boldness because of the *Brown* decision to seek freedom at any cost, even under the threat of death. In Mississippi, the ugliness of racial hatred reached a boiling point. Because the national media covered the events in the South, the world saw firsthand how bad things really were. They saw how far racist whites would go to maintain their sacred rules of racial separation. Mississippi was one of the hotbeds of racial unrest.

In 1955, a minister was lynched after he led a voter registration drive in Belzoni, Mississippi, and another man was killed in Brookhaven, Mississippi. In August of that same year, Emmett Till, a fourteen-year-old black boy from Chicago visiting his Mississippi cousins, was beaten, mutilated, and shot in the head for saying "Bye baby" to a white woman or, as some have recalled, whistling to her as he left a country store in Money, Mississippi. His body was thrown in the Tallahassee River. The woman's husband and her brother-in-law were arrested for the murder, but an all-white male jury in Somers, Mississippi, acquitted the men. The world gasped when they saw the boy's disfigured body lying in an open casket. His mother wanted the world to see what had been done to her son.

The brazen and brutal murder of Emmett Till sent fear through the black community like no other killing had. Blacks still talked about it when I was growing up. I remember my Granny sternly warning my brothers never to look at or talk to a white girl or woman.

A few miles from where we lived was the town of Pocahontas, which had two country stores that were owned by whites. Granny didn't have a car, but she walked to Pocahontas several times a day to buy—on credit—items that she needed to cook dinner. She never got everything she needed in one trip. She always forgot something and had to go back several times a day. This was a treat for us because Granny was fun to be around and we liked going places with her. There was nothing else better to do in rural Mississippi. Besides, she sometimes bought us a goody.

One time, when Granny took my oldest brother to the store with her, one of the owner's daughters was playing outside. When she saw my brother, she asked him if he wanted a bite of her cinnamon roll. Granny overheard the girl and pulled my brother away. On the way home, Granny told him to stay away from that girl unless he wanted to end up murdered like Emmett Till.

Granny knew the drill. First the Klan would burn a cross on your front lawn as a warning. Then they would come back later and drag the men, kicking and screaming, out of the house and hang them on a tree.

No matter how shocking Emmet Till's brazen murder was, some white Mississippians still supported the killers and the state's so-called Southern way of life. Mississippi Governor Ross Barnett proudly declared that segregation was Mississippi's heritage, and that he would do everything in his power to ensure that blacks and whites lived separate lives. Whites tried to prevent racial integration by instilling fear in the black population.

Segregated Buses

The violence that whites unleashed on blacks did little to stop their march to freedom. In November 1955, the Interstate Commerce Commission (ICC) banned segregation on interstate buses. But in the South, interstate as well as public city buses were still segregated. Most Southern cities had laws that reserved the first few rows of seats in city buses for whites. If the reserved seats were filled, then blacks had to give up their seats in the back to accommodate white passengers.

In December 1955, Rosa Parks, a seamstress, sat in the black section of a Montgomery, Alabama, city bus. When the bus driver asked Parks and other black passengers to give up their seats for white passengers, she refused and was arrested. Parks was no ordinary citizen; she was an active and vocal member of the local NAACP and had served as secretary of the Montgomery chapter. This was also not the first time she had refused to give up her seat to a white person.

In protest, black leaders organized a one-day bus boycott, but when the city refused to negotiate, the community decided to continue it indefinitely. The Reverand Martin Luther King, Jr., a young Baptist minister new to Montgomery (he was pastor of Dexter Avenue Baptist Church), was chosen to lead the movement.

During the boycott, blacks either walked to work or arranged rides with other blacks who owned cars. In addition, some white women who needed black maids to clean their houses, cook their meals, and provide childcare picked up and dropped off their domestic help. Most whites did not want to give up the customs that had been in force since the early 1600s, when slaves were first brought to this country. In the South, blacks were not considered citizens and had always been denied benefits that whites enjoyed. Blacks served whites in every facet of Southern life and whites refused to give up their privileged stature.

Racists in Alabama unleashed a wave of violence on black leaders. The home of the Reverand Fred Shuttlesworth, an outspoken Baptist minister from Birmingham, was bombed. King's home was also bombed. A grand jury indicted black leaders, charging them with conducting an illegal boycott. The NAACP took the case to federal court. The state also banned the NAACP from operating in Montgomery, a ban that lasted almost a decade.

The boycott ended on December 21, 1956, when a federal court ruled that Montgomery bus segregation was unconstitutional. The city appealed to the U.S. Supreme Court, which upheld the ruling. Whites who were upset about the ruling went on a shooting spree, targeting black ministers, including King, and the integrated city buses.

In March 1956, the so-called Southern Manifesto, signed by nineteen Southern senators and eighty-one Southern representatives, was presented to Congress. These politicians blamed the Supreme Court for the *Brown* decision, which they said was destroying the good relations between black and white Southerners. The manifesto called activists who sought school integration "outside agitators." Its signers felt like the federal government was usurping state rights.

Because the Montgomery bus boycott was successful, black ministers established the Atlanta-based Southern Christian Leadership Conference (SCLC) in 1957 and chose Martin Luther King to lead it. The group represented a coalition of community civil rights leaders, mostly black Baptist ministers, in the South. SCLC was determined to fight segregation and register black voters in the Deep South.

In 1957, Congress passed a civil rights act that guaranteed everyone the right to vote. It also created the U.S. Commission on Civil Rights, which had the power to investigate voting abuses.

Meanwhile, students in the Deep South were fighting segregated education.

School Desegregation

Blacks in my community didn't try to force their way into all-white schools. Their fear was too great. They knew what would happen if they tried to mingle with whites. Most Northern and some Southern states desegregated their schools, but the Deep South refused. In states where black students tried to integrate public schools and colleges, violence erupted.

In February 1956, after Autherine Lucy enrolled at the all-white University of Alabama under federal court order, students and local whites rioted. School officials temporarily suspended her, for her own protection they said. She sued to get reinstated, but the school eventually forced her out permanently.

In 1957, in Little Rock, Arkansas, nine black teenagers were chosen to integrate Central High School after the school board designed a desegregation plan to comply with the *Brown* decision. In response, Arkansas Governor Orval Faubus called up the National Guard to prevent the students from entering the school on the day the Supreme Court ordered Central High School to integrate. When eight of the students and the adults with them arrived, the guards turned them away, refusing to let them enter the school. The ninth student, a girl, had walked to school alone and she met a mob of angry whites who hurled derogatory insults at her. A white woman came to the girl's rescue and escorted her to a city bus.

President Dwight Eisenhower convinced Faubus to let the "Little Rock Nine" enter the school, but when Faubus sent police officers to the school, angry white protesters turned on the police and fought them until they removed the black students from the school.

After the state of Arkansas overstepped Eisenhower's authority, he sent federal troops in to enforce integration at Central High School. Each black student had a soldier who escorted him or her to class every day.

On May 29, 1958, 601 white students and one black student graduated from Central High. The next year, the governor closed all city schools so they would not have to integrate. The state of Virginia followed suit. In 1960 in New Orleans, riots broke out when four little black girls went to first grade in an all-white school.

White colleges were also targeted for integration. In 1961, James Meredith, a native Mississippian, applied to enter the University of Mississippi ("Ole Miss") in Oxford. After serving nine years in the U.S. Air Force, he had returned home in 1960. When the school found out he was black, it refused his application. Meredith, represented by the NAACP, filed suit in a U.S. district court. The judge ruled in favor of the school and Meredith appealed the decision. In June 1962, the Court of Appeals ruled that Ole Miss had to accept Meredith. Mississippi appealed to the U.S. Supreme Court, which upheld the lower court's ruling. Mississippi Governor Ross Barnett, who was also an attorney, said that no school in Mississippi would be integrated while he was governor. The board of trustees supported Barnett, who epitomized racism and white supremacy in Mississippi. Quoting from a 1962 edition of the *Hartford Courant*, Fred Powledge, author of *Free at Last? The Civil Rights Movement and the People Who Made It*, gave a scathing account of Barnett's true character.

> When [Ross Barnett] was in Connecticut in 1950 trying a damage suit for a construction worker, Barnett became incensed when he discovered that a Negro was eating in the same restaurant with him. He demanded that the owner throw the Negro out. The owner refused, and Barnett, said the newspaper, became so abusive that the proprietor called the police, who took Barnett into custody. He was released without charge after apologizing to the restaurant owner.

On September 20, 1961, Barnett stood at the entrance of Ole Miss and blocked Meredith from entering. Five days later, at the state office building in Jackson, Meredith, accompanied by an attorney from the U.S. Justice Department, again tried to register. Barnett was there waiting and refused him admission, saying he was trying to maintain the "Southern way of life."

In Washington, President John F. Kennedy worked to find a way that would force the state of Mississippi to allow Meredith to enroll in the college. On September 30, 1961, Kennedy ordered U.S. marshals to the state to prepare for Meredith's arrival. Meredith was flown into Oxford in north central Mississippi, not far from Memphis, and taken to a secret location.

Later that night, when Kennedy went on national television to tell the nation what was taking place at Ole Miss, the campus became a war zone. The federal marshals stood by while protesters hurled bricks and other objects at them. The media were also physically attacked. Two people were killed and more than 300 were injured. The Mississippi National Guard was sent in to help the federal officers. The Army was sent in to restore order and James Meredith was eventually allowed to register. He graduated from Ole Miss on August 18, 1963.

Freedom Rides

In 1961, blacks in some states still had to sit in the back of city buses and were not allowed to sit in the bus stations' whites-only waiting rooms. Black leaders pressured the Kennedy administration to force Southern states, through the ICC, to demand that buses be integrated.

When Kennedy did nothing, CORE, which had been organized in 1942, began Freedom Rides. They recruited both white and black protestors to ride buses together through the South. On May 4, 1961, seven black and six white Freedom Riders boarded two buses in Washington, D.C., and headed south, to travel through Greensboro, North Carolina; Rock Hill, South Carolina; Atlanta, Georgia; Anniston, Birmingham, and Montgomery, Alabama; Jackson, Mississippi; and New Orleans, Louisiana.

Before these protestors boarded the designated Greyhound and Trailways buses, they participated in nonviolence workshops. On May 4, black volunteers sat in the front of the buses and white volunteers sat in the back, and they all refused to move when ordered. When they arrived at bus stations, white protesters sat in blacks-only waiting rooms and black riders went into whites-only waiting rooms. During a stop in South Carolina, two of the riders were attacked by angry whites.

On May 14, the group left Atlanta for Birmingham, still on two buses. They met little resistance until they got to Anniston where a Klan mob was waiting. The mob blocked the bus exits and the bus pulled away with a throng of angry whites following it. Just outside of Anniston, Klan members tried to get on the bus but Alabama state police stopped them. Someone bombed the Greyhound bus and destroyed it. Twelve riders were hospitalized and treated for smoke inhalation.

The mob waited for the Trailways bus to arrive in Anniston, and they beat those passengers. When the bus arrived in Birmingham, another mob was waiting to attack. A white pro-desegregation demonstrator was beaten unconscious and hospitalized.

The notorious Eugene "Bull" Connor, Birmingham's public safety commissioner, was criticized for not providing the riders with police protection. Black leaders had asked the FBI for protection, but they received no help. The bureau failed to notify other federal officials that it had advance information from KKK sources that mobs would attack the riders in Birmingham and that police would not stop them.

Because of the violence, Greyhound bus drivers refused to take the Freedom Riders to Montgomery, Alabama's capital city, so President Kennedy intervened and asked Alabama Governor John Patterson to provide protection for the demonstrators. Patterson first agreed but then changed his mind, calling the riders "fools and agitators." Finally, the CORE volunteers took an airplane to their final destination in New Orleans.

CORE ended the rides, but Student Nonviolent Coordinating Committee (SNCC; a group created in 1960 by college students who participated in sit-ins in the South) members from Nashville decided that the Freedom Rides should continue. On May 17, 1961, a new group of riders from Nashville arrived in Birmingham to a waiting mob. The riders, eight blacks and two whites, including civil rights movement leader and Birmingham minister, Fred Shuttlesworth, were arrested. They were charged with conspiracy to cause a mob to gather and with disturbing the peace. Some posted bail and left.

Governor Patterson asked a state circuit judge to ban the riders from coming into Alabama. Police stopped buses entering the state and read the injunction. People from all over the country who were sympathetic to the riders rode buses to Montgomery and were arrested for integrating bus terminals. Reverand William Sloane Coffin, Jr., Yale University's chaplain, spent a night in jail. President Kennedy and his brother, Attorney General Robert Kennedy, tried to contact Patterson by phone and ask him to restore order in his state but Patterson refused to speak with them.

Meanwhile, Bull Connor went to the jail, released the demonstrators, and personally returned them in police cars to the

Tennessee border. The students were not deterred in their mission. They found rides back to Birmingham so that they could continue their journey. They had great difficulty finding a bus that would take them to Montgomery. Robert Kennedy was contacted and he called the president of Greyhound and asked him to find a driver for the Freedom Riders. He also called Governor Patterson, who still refused to discuss the issue. Robert Kennedy sent a federal special assistant to Alabama to meet with Patterson and obtain a guarantee that the riders would not be injured. Patterson would not agree, but the director of Alabama public safety said he could assure their safety. Supposedly an arrangement was worked out among the U.S. Justice Department, Greyhound officials, and the state of Alabama. A private plane would fly over the bus and highway patrol cars would be parked along the highway from Birmingham to Montgomery, which is about ninety miles away.

Unfortunately, outside of Montgomery, the plane and patrol cars disappeared. Even though the FBI had warned Montgomery officials that violence would break out, there were no police officers at the bus terminal. Local officials had promised that they could handle any problems that arose. But when the bus pulled into Montgomery, whites with sticks and bricks yelled, "Nigger, kill the niggers." The attackers savagely beat the Freedom Riders, especially the whites. Police arrested the demonstrators for violating the injunction against Freedom Rides.

President Kennedy asked the federal court in Montgomery to stop the Klan and any other people from interfering with interstate travel by bus, and he asked the FBI to send more investigators to the city. Robert Kennedy sent U.S. marshals to an Air Force base outside of Montgomery to help enforce the law. This move incensed Governor Patterson, who accused the federal government of interfering in a domestic state matter, which he said Washington helped create.

When the marshals arrived, Martin Luther King flew in to lead a rally at the First Baptist Church, where Reverand Ralph Abernathy, the pastor, was also the main speaker. Most of the nation's civil rights leaders were there to support the Freedom Riders. An angry group surrounded the church and threatened those inside, but the federal marshals kept the mob from going inside the church. Outside, rioting whites burned cars and attacked the marshals. King called Robert Kennedy and reported the situation. Kennedy called Governor Patterson and demanded that the civil rights leaders be protected, but Patterson said he could not protect them. Federal marshals told the rally participants to spend the night in the church.

When tear gas seeped inside the church, King calmed the crowd and told them not to be afraid. He vowed to continue to stand up for what is right. Some whites in Alabama had a difficult time accepting that the activists would not give up their fight for freedom. As the violence exploded outside the church, Governor Patterson declared marshal law and sent in state police and the Alabama National Guard.

Robert Kennedy asked the Freedom Riders to stop the rides and take some time to cool off, but they refused. In late May 1961, with National Guardsmen around the Montgomery bus terminal, the Freedom Riders left for Jackson, Mississippi.

The Jackson Nonviolent Movement (JNM), an offshoot of SNCC, helped coordinate housing for the Freedom Riders in Mississippi. They also planned mass meetings at area churches, conducted voter registration, and ran nonviolent protest workshops. In 1961, they picketed Mississippi's segregated state fair. JNM also provided free literature and tapes of Dr. King's speeches, sold recordings of protest music, showed movement films at churches, and published a newsletter called *Voice of the Jackson Movement*.

On the way to Mississippi, some guards rode on the bus, helicopters flew overhead, and state police cars drove in front and in back of the bus. Mississippi National Guardsmen were stationed on the highway. At the Jackson bus station in the magnolia state, two busloads with a total of twenty-seven Freedom Riders were escorted through the Trailways bus terminal and arrested; they were charged with breach of peace and refusing to obey an officer. Police took them to jail in paddy wagons.

By the end of 1961, more than 300 people, mostly college students, had been arrested during Freedom Rides, but Greyhound quietly desegregated its bus terminal in Montgomery.

It was later learned that Robert Kennedy had made a deal with Mississippi authorities. In return for no violence, Kennedy did not enforce the U.S. Supreme Court ruling that public facilities must be integrated. In court, the Freedom Riders were convicted and fined 200 dollars each. They received sixty days in Parchman State Penitentiary, a maximum-security prison.*

While police continued to arrest blacks who participated in direct action to force integration, CORE kept pressure on President Kennedy to enforce the higher court ruling that banned segregation in interstate travel, which was being ignored in the South. In the summer of 1961, hundreds of Freedom Riders were arrested, and finally Robert Kennedy asked the ICC to enforce the ban on segregation in interstate travel. On September 22, 1961, the ICC complied.

Demonstrations versus Segregation

SNCC members went to Albany, Georgia, a center of white resistance, to help blacks fight segregation. They went to the Trailways bus station to see if local police would arrest them, which they did. Albany officials refused to obey the ban on segregated interstate transportation.

---

* Parchman state prison is well known in Mississippi and greatly feared by black people. Most of the men incarcerated there are black. When I was a young girl, prisoners in black-and-white jumpsuits were brought in ankle chains to work on the dirt road we lived on. They would clear brush and dig out the debris from ditches. We would watch them work while white men with shotguns sat on the big trucks and watched them work also. We couldn't go near them, but sometimes they made eye contact with us and their eyes seemed so sad. It was like they were embarrassed for us to see them like that. Sometimes I thought about running over and grabbing those white men's guns, so that the black men could run away. But Mama warned us never to go near them. She was afraid they would hurt us.

When we did something really bad, Mama would whip us with switches and say, "I'm whipping you now so the white man won't kill you later." If you did something bad and the whites put you in prison, they would put you "on the backside of Pentation," Mama used to say. The grownups never said penitentiary; they called it *pentation*. I have no idea what the backside of it was, but Mama made it sound awful, a place where no one wanted to go.

On a few of my visits home as a college student, I went with a friend who was visiting a relative at Parchman. I saw black men working in the sprawling cotton fields on the surrounding plantations. While living in Milwaukee, I visited a state prison with my cousin. I saw men lifting weights, playing cards, and reading books, some for college courses. I didn't see any of this at Parchman.

In October 1961, SNCC began a voter registration project in southwest Georgia. Earlier that year, blacks had asked the city to desegregate its facilities and city officials refused. Instead of challenging the city with sit-ins and forced integration, SNCC decided to register blacks to vote. But blacks' fear was too entrenched in the segregated society of the racist South.

In November 1961, members of SNCC and the local NAACP, ministers, and some others formed the Albany Movement. The movement held mass meetings and led marches from black neighborhoods to downtown to protest at city hall, where they usually kneeled and prayed. The police would arrest them.

Martin Luther King and the SCLC came to help the Albany Movement. King led a march to downtown and was arrested. Albany Police Chief Pritchett had a plan: in some Southern cities, when the jails filled up, protestors were released. But Chief Pritchett had read King's writings and knew about his strategy of filling up city jails. He outsmarted King and other civil rights leaders by not letting the city jails fill up; he sent demonstrators to nearby county jails. Whites in Albany dug in their heels and aggressively went after blacks who tried to break open its segregated society. When blacks boycotted the city bus line, businessmen who stood to lose money made an agreement with the Albany Movement and the bus company to integrate city buses and hire black drivers. Because city officials did not support the agreement, the bus company shut down.

After being arrested four months earlier for parading without a permit, King and the Reverand Ralph Abernathy went to trial in July 1962; the judge sentenced them to forty-five days in jail. Three days later, they were released. Someone had secretly paid their fines. The police chief had studied King's writings and knew his strategy; he also knew there would be violence whenever King was in jail.

Still, the city commission refused to meet with members of the Albany Movement to discuss the racial unrest because city officials considered them violators of the law. Movement members began preparing lawsuits to challenge Albany's segregated public facilities, where blacks were turned away at the library, pool, and park. But the courts did little to help because most of the judges were also racist segregationists.

That summer, the city asked a federal judge to issue a restraining order to end the nine-month long demonstrations. The judge issued a temporary restraining order against the Albany Movement. King said he would obey the injunction because it was temporary. SNCC members disagreed.

A federal district judge overturned the temporary injunction, saying it denied free speech. King and Abernathy led a group to city hall to meet with the city commission and were arrested. The federal judge who had issued the temporary injunction held a hearing for a permanent injunction on demonstrations against segregation. City officials decided to meet with hand-picked blacks to discuss race relations in Albany.

King left Albany after the movement failed to integrate the city. His influence and tenacity were powerful in changing unjust laws in most Southern cities, but he failed to change the minds of hardened bigots in that small town. SNCC continued demonstrating and police kept arresting them. The wife of a civil rights leader in Albany was nine months pregnant and had her three young children with her when she visited some young, jailed protesters to bring them food. A prison guard yelled at her and some other women to move away from the prison fence, and when she turned to say something to him, he beat her on the head until she was unconscious. She lost the baby.

SNCC recruited Northern white college students to help push the cause and they also began a voter registration drive. King and the SCLC went to Birmingham, the largest city in Alabama.

Birmingham

In Birmingham, King and his group faced one of their most vicious challenges in the movement—Alabama Governor George C. Wallace. In January 1963, Wallace, the symbol of the South's white resistance, had stood on the steps of the capitol and delivered his inaugural speech, bellowing out to a cheering crowd, "Segregation now, segregation tomorrow, segregation forever."

Birmingham was nicknamed "Bombingham" because of the large number of bombing attacks there. While the violence raged, public safety commissioner Bull Connor stood by and did nothing.

He had been elected to six terms, and as overseer of the police department, he had ordered direct attacks on blacks. He was racist to his core and did not try to hide it.

Connor was not the only staunch segregationist in town. When a federal court ordered the city to integrate its public facilities, city officials responded by closing its parks, playgrounds, swimming pools, and golf courses. At the time, white supremacists believed that if blacks and whites mingled together, they would produce a race of "mongrel" children.

By 1963, both blacks and whites were tired of Connor and his posse and wanted a change in Birmingham. A group of people who represented businesses and civic organizations met and decided to change the corrupt city government through initiative. They first petitioned for a referendum by gathering a certain number of signatures. After winning the referendum, an election date was set for April 1963 to select a new city government. Connor tried to keep power by running for mayor, but he lost to a racial moderate. The old city government refused to leave without a fight; they wanted to serve out their terms, which would have ended in 1965. The newly elected officials sued the defeated ones.

Meanwhile, SCLC launched a project at the 16th Street Baptist Church, which served as the movement's headquarters. On the first day of a protest, twenty-one demonstrators were arrested. This was not the first time that Birmingham's blacks had challenged the segregated system. In 1956, the Reverand Fred Shuttlesworth, a Baptist minister from Birmingham, and others had demanded the desegregation of city buses. His house and church were bombed as he slept. A year later, when Shuttlesworth tried to enroll his children in an all-white school, he was attacked and beaten.

The city government was in limbo, and whites were growing tired of the demonstrations and wanted them to cease. The city went to court and got an injunction from the state court to end the demonstrations.

Martin Luther King came to Birmingham in April 1963, and organized demonstrations in the city and disrupted the shopping season, which upset business owners. The owners decided to integrate their stores, which meant that the "Whites Only" and "Blacks Only" signs would be removed from restaurants, bathrooms, water fountains, and fitting rooms, and to hire blacks to work at their businesses. Segregationists fought this change.

During a march on Good Friday, King was arrested for parading without a permit. President Kennedy called King's wife, Coretta, and told her that the FBI had been directed to make sure King would not be mistreated in jail. While he was locked up, some local white ministers released a statement criticizing King and the movement's actions. They called for an end to the demonstrations and urged local blacks to withdraw from the protests. The clergy considered King a troublemaker who sought publicity.

In solitary confinement, King wrote his moving Letter from a Birmingham Jail. "Justice too long delayed, is justice denied," wrote King, responding to the white clergy. He stated that black people had waited too long for equal rights that had been stymied by segregation. He believed that nonviolent action was the only way to get white people's attention and force change, and that it was okay to violate laws when they were unjust. King faulted the white clergy for taking a back seat instead of being leaders in the fight for justice for all people.

Finally, the mayor and a new city council were sworn in, but the old commissioners would not allow the newly elected government to be seated. Birmingham had two governments; each one met at different times to conduct city business. Bull Connor remained in charge of the police and fire department until the courts decided which government was legal.

The demonstrations lost support while King sat in jail. When King was released on bond, thousands of children skipped school to march in Birmingham. Police arrested hundreds of children and jailed them. Bull Conner tried to stop the marches before they began and brought out police dogs. He also called in the fire department and ordered it to turn fire hoses on the demonstrators. The water pressure was so powerful that it stripped the bark off of trees. National media exposure of the events shocked the world. The federal government worried about America's image around the world, but George Wallace saw it differently. He said the world should be concerned about what Alabamans thought of them because of the foreign aid America sends to poor countries.

Demonstrators kept marching and some turned violent. Thousands of black children were arrested. Connor ordered more hoses turned on them and the world saw small bodies being lifted in the air by the powerful pressure from the water hoses.

Jails filled to capacity. The U.S. Justice Department tried to mediate an agreement between the demonstrators and the city. Blacks and whites physically fought each other in downtown Birmingham.

After weeks of fighting, some of the city's black and white leaders reached a resolution and on May 9 announced an agreement to integrate lunch counters and push for the hiring of more black people. The KKK did not accept the agreement and set off a bomb in a hotel outside the room where King had been staying (he had already left). When a crowd gathered by the hotel, police beat the people back with clubs. Some of the people rioted, burning police cars and several buildings.

The case of the two city governments in Alabama soon reached the U.S. Supreme Court and in May, the Court ruled that the newly elected city government was the legitimate one. The officials were finally seated. The Court also banned Birmingham's segregation laws.

Governor Wallace continued to put up a fight. On June 11, 1963, with state troopers in force, Wallace made a show of standing in the doorway of a building at the University of Alabama's Tuscaloosa campus and stopping two black students from entering the school under a federal court order. He made a speech before leaving to allow the students entrance.

The Struggle Continues

As the cemented walls of segregation steadily crumbled, Southern white leaders vehemently fought to keep them intact. At the same time, blacks began to become more militant.

Riots broke out in other cities and racial tensions gripped the country. Unrest spread to the North and people protested in the streets.

President Kennedy took a stronger position than any president had since Lincoln, saying that no city or state could ignore the cries for equality. He asked Congress to pass a civil rights bill.

Martin Luther King called for a mass march on Washington, D.C., to demonstrate for jobs, voting rights, and freedom. More than 200,000 people attended the march on August 28, 1963, and stood on the mall between the Washington Monument and the Lincoln Memorial. Black and white activists, labor leaders, clergy, and celebrities came. They walked or came on buses or trains.

Security was tight to prevent violence. Several black leaders spoke at the march, including the chairman of SNCC, John Lewis, who had to change his speech because it was critical of President Kennedy's civil rights bill, which Lewis said lacked police protection for black protesters. This is also where Martin Luther King gave his famous "I Have a Dream" speech.

> When we allow freedom to ring from every village and every hamlet, from every state and every city, we will be able to speed up that day when all of God's children, black men and white men, Jews and Gentiles, Protestants and Catholics, will be able to join hands and sing the words of the old Negro Spiritual, Free at last, free at last, thank God Almighty, we're free at last.

That march effectively made King the leader of the civil rights movement.

White racists weren't giving up. On Sunday, September 15, 1963, shortly after the March on Washington, a bomb exploded at the 16th Street Baptist Church in Birmingham, the headquarters of King's SCLC, before the service began on that morning. Several people were injured and four young black girls were killed: two were teenagers and two were preteens. Blacks refused to give up. As they buried the girls, mourners sang, "We shall overcome, we shall overcome, we shall overcome some day. Deep in my heart, I do believe, we shall overcome some day."

In Washington, FBI Chief J. Edgar Hoover convinced the Kennedy administration that communists had infiltrated the civil rights movement and Attorney General Robert Kennedy approved temporary taps on King's telephones. On November 22, 1963, President Kennedy was assassinated in Dallas, and in the aftermath, the taps continued unnoticed.

Although Kennedy was a white man, his death saddened Daddy, Mama, and Granny because they said he had tried to help blacks.

My Schools

"Mother wit is better than book learning," Granny used to say. "There's no bigger fool than an educated fool."

By 1955, the Supreme Court had established guidelines for desegregating schools, but these made little difference to blacks. Because we lived in "the country," the county government had jurisdiction over rural properties. Besides, there were no elementary schools in the area for blacks.

Black churches filled the gap by setting up schools on their property. My older brothers and sisters attended one of these church schools, Whitfield School at Pine Grove Missionary Baptist Church. School was open Monday through Friday, for grades first through fifth. It was located in a white wooden building in back of Pine Grove Church on Old Highway 49. Daddy said it had opened in the 1930s and that the school was named for a white family, the Whitfields, who had sold the church the land.

My sister Ora recalls that the school had four rooms with a wood stove that served as a source of heat. There were four teachers and about twenty students who used hand-me-down books from a white school. The teachers taught reading, writing, and arithmetic and during recess, the children made jump ropes from tree vines. The children brought their lunches to school and stored them in a cabinet. Some of the teachers sold coconut cookies—two for a penny. Outside there was a cistern and two outhouses—one for girls and one for boys—behind the school. Each morning the children said the Lord's Prayer and the Pledge of Allegiance. School ended in May so the children could work in the fields.

Once, before I was old enough to attend school, Mama dropped me off at Whitfield School to stay with my older sisters while she went to do errands. Mama knew the teacher, who went to our church next door. Back then, everyone pitched in to help each other;

Frankye's sister Ora in July 1971. Author's original family photograph.

we were a community. Mama didn't hesitate because she knew I would be well taken care of. The older kids played with and doted on me. I was queen for a day. I remember the school was stark white with a steeple that had a bell inside.

Thinking of that old chalky white school reminds me of a funny story about Granny. One Sunday she visited the church next door to the school. She had to pee and I went to the outhouse with her and stood in front of the door so that no one would walk in on her. A few minutes later Granny ran out with her bloomers wrapped around her ankles, almost knocking me over. She had been squatting down when she looked up and saw a big snake coiled above the doorway. I teased her about that for years.

The family's Shetland pony and Ora standing next to the house in Mississippi in 1972. Aunt Maggie's (Daddy's sister) house is in the background. Author's original family photograph.

The county eventually built an elementary school for rural blacks, because officials knew that the courts would eventually force them to integrate schools after the *Brown* decision. Lovett Elementary School opened in 1963 in nearby Clinton, Mississippi. Ten years earlier, Sumner Hill, the first high school for blacks in the area where my family lived, had been built in the same town.

Clinton was known back then as one of the bastions of racial hatred in Mississippi. Folks told us to be on our "P's and Q's" because the Grand Wizard of the Mississippi Ku Klux Klan supposedly lived there. There was a sandy, dirt, and rock road in Clinton that everyone called Sand Road. At the end of Sand Road was Sand Hill, the place where the Klan allegedly hung black men and left them dangling on ropes tied in tall trees as examples to keep blacks in their place. Parents and teachers warned us never to set foot on Sand Hill. Folks were afraid even to talk about it, except for a seventh-grade English teacher who told us stories about headless bodies dangling from tree limbs and bloodstains crying out of the ground for help. Older kids bragged about sneaking down there and hearing muffled sounds. I was too afraid to set foot on Sand Hill and never went there.

In my elementary school, the students, teachers, principal, and bus drivers were black. Our parents knew most of them from church. If a child acted up in church on Sunday, a teacher would punish him or her in school on Monday. I didn't get in much trouble and never got punished at school because I knew the teachers would tell Mama and Daddy. My fourth-grade teacher, Miss Ford, used to tell me to ask Daddy to send her some hog sausage whenever he killed a pig. I was embarrassed when she said that out loud in class, but as long as I had something she wanted, it kept me out of trouble.

Mississippi schools remained segregated well after the U.S. Supreme Court ruled segregation unconstitutional in its *Brown v. Board of Education* decision in 1954. Whites with money fled cities and towns and built their own communities and schools, barring black kids from enrolling in them.

Black teachers could not effectively educate black children without the same resources white children had. If everything had been equal in that respect, then we wouldn't have needed forced busing to integrate the schools. I remember how embarrassed our teachers were when they handed out used books that white schools had delivered to us. Our teachers taped the torn covers and scratched the white kids' names off of the books so that we could write our own names in them. The teachers instructed us not to get molasses on our books at home. We had to keep them in good shape for the class who would use them the following school year.

I didn't see a white face in my school until 1973, when I was in seventh grade. A federal judge ordered forced busing to integrate schools and make them equal. Whites were in an uproar over the prospect of having black children in "their" schools. Forced busing, while conceived with good intentions, was handled poorly. Schools were redistricted and some black children were uprooted from their familiar schools and surroundings and thrown into hostile white schools.

A few white teachers were sent to our school, and a few black teachers went to white schools, but no white children were bused to our school. Nor did our education improve because state education officials sent us white teachers who didn't make the grade at white schools. Our school was still as segregated and inferior as it was before the Court intervened.

Rumors ran rampant about what would happen to the defenseless black children who were so out of place at predominately white schools. I was sure they would be beaten and possibly killed; I was surprised when there was little violence. Race relations slowly improved and students were gradually accepted.

Our so-called public school integration went fairly well considering Mississippi's history of violence. A picnic area was created at the Madison County reservoir and named after Ross Barnett, the governor who refused to let James Meredith enroll at Ole Miss. After high school graduations, it was a ritual back then for black classes to go there and celebrate. But I have never been there; I refuse to go.

Although forced busing didn't trigger riots at the Clinton schools, it did in the North. There were riots in Boston when a federal judge ordered its public schools to desegregate in 1974. I saw whites attacking black students who were trying to enter predominately white schools—I remember a photo of a white man shoving an American flag into a black man's stomach. I had been led to believe that it was only whites in the South who were racists and denied blacks a decent education. I realized then that there were some whites in the North who were as racist as those in the South.

In 1975 I went to a combined junior and high school. Most of my teachers were white, but the school still had no white students. I didn't think it was necessary for us to go to school with white kids to get a good education, but I knew if whites were forced to attend our school, the state would provide better qualified teachers and educational materials. Of course we would have been better off if the state had provided a quality education for all students, regardless of color, but state officials really didn't care about educating black children.

Some of the white teachers who were sent to my school didn't attempt to hide their disgust at having to teach black children. One time, a white home economics teacher became enraged at me and some other girls for burning a peach pie in cooking class. We didn't do it on purpose and told her it was an accident. She yelled, "I would rather be digging ditches than come back here next year." She must have found that ditch-digging job because she didn't return the next school year. We never saw her again.

She wasn't the only one who was not interested in helping us learn. There was a math teacher whom we called a redneck because he never wanted us to touch him when we handed in our papers. He was hot-tempered and mean. When he got mad at us, usually for no good reason, his face would turn red and he would storm out of the classroom and chain smoke. We laughed at the way he walked because the back of his knees and his calves bent so far back that they looked as if they were going to break. He walked like Shaggy on the television show *Scooby-Doo*. He had short black hair with a part on the side and he had a nervous habit of running his fingers through it from one side to the other.

One year I had the flu and Mama kept me home for two weeks. When I returned to school a few weeks before final exams, I was so behind in algebra that there was no way I could catch up without being tutored. The math teacher gave me a choice: I could either accept the grade I had before I got sick—an A—or I could take the final and risk failing the course. I opted for the A, but I never caught up in math. The next year, whenever my new math teacher called on me for an answer in class or asked me to come up to the blackboard to work a problem, I panicked. Even though I had always been good in math, I fell so far behind my classmates that I became frustrated and too embarrassed to ask them for help. We didn't have tutors and I wasn't comfortable asking my teachers for extra help, especially because they didn't want to be there in the first place.

The math teacher's only redeeming quality was he married an English teacher whom all the students were fond of. She was white but a good-hearted person, warm and compassionate. She never yelled or screamed at us and we couldn't understand why she married him. When they came to our school, they were married to other people. They had a romance that everyone knew about, but they tried to hide it from us. They would sneak into the teachers' lounge when it was empty and come out with red faces and tousled hair. They denied their affair until they finally divorced their spouses and married each other. We thought it was funny how they pretended to have high moral standards.

After he married that English teacher, the math teacher tried to change his racist attitudes. He began offering to share his lunch with us. One time he asked the class if anyone wanted an egg sandwich he had bought and brought to school. It was wrapped tightly in a clear plastic wrap. "It hasn't been touched by human hands," he said proudly. Someone asked him, "If no one touched it, then who made the sandwich and wrapped it?" No one ever took food from him.

Not all the white teachers at my school were openly racist. One English teacher, Mr. Luby, treated us decently, although we sometimes gave him a hard time because of the way the others treated us; it took us a long time to see that he was sincere about teaching us. When he tried being nice, we talked back to him and wouldn't listen in class. One time he threw up his hands and stormed out of the classroom after we brought him to tears. He thought he was trying to do a good thing and we acted like the children we were.

One day he told us that his parents were racists and would never allow a black person to set foot in their house. Mr. Luby frequently took a bunch of kids to his house in Clinton. I guess he thought he could make a difference by doing everything his parents hated. He brought treats to school for us, and on weekends, he took some students to the movies. Of course, Mama and Daddy never let me go.

Mr. Luby pulled me aside one day and apologized for the school not having honor classes that I could attend. He said he could tell I was bored with school and needed something more. I was surprised because I didn't realize anyone noticed. A scholarship would help me go to college, he said, but there were none set aside for our school. Most of the academic scholarships went to white kids. I suppose educators assumed black children were inferior. I didn't believe that. I knew I was smart enough to compete with white kids for scholarships.

It wasn't until I enrolled in a university up North that I discovered Mississippi schools had not prepared me for college work. Even then, I hadn't fully figured out I was unprepared; I thought the work was too hard. I probably should have taken refresher courses before jumping in, but I didn't want to start over. I refused to give up and allow my past to defeat me, and for years I worked hard until I earned a bachelor's degree. The one thing that came easy for me was writing.

In high school, Mr. Luby showed interest in my poetry after I let him read my collection of poems. I didn't feel comfortable letting others read my work, but for some reason I let him critique it. He said my writing reminded him of Edna St. Vincent Millay's work, and he gave me a book of her poetry. I had never heard of her before and when I read her poetry, I wasn't impressed. Although I was enchanted with romanticism, I was more into Edgar Allan Poe and his melancholic writing. Mr. Luby kept critiquing my work and told me my talent for writing needed to be cultivated and that I should write every day.

One older black teacher didn't like how Mr. Luby spent so much time with me and other black students. This is the same teacher who told students about the lynchings on Sand Road in Clinton. One time, when Mr. Luby took some students to the movies, they ran into her and he gave her a big hug. The black teacher told Mr. Luby never to do that again as long as he lived. I guess she still had angry feelings about whites, too many memories, and too much pain. Supposedly, some whites had hanged a relative of hers on Sand Road.

I went through a transformation in high school. I became popular and hung out with both the nerds and the troublemakers. The jocks were my best friends and they looked after and protected me. I was too smart to get into trouble, and too quiet for the teachers to suspect that I did. The invisible child blossomed.

I became my friends' psychologist. I was cool and collected. I didn't smile and I didn't cry. Cool people didn't show emotions. Because I read a lot, I thought I knew everything about everything. Not only did I read books, but I also read *Life, Ebony, Jet,* and *Teen* magazines so I knew all about the movie stars' business. There was nothing I didn't know about the Jackson Five. I even sneaked my brothers' dirty magazines from under their mattresses and read them, too. When my classmates asked questions about sex, I proudly quoted stuff I had read. Nothing was off limits. When we got into discussions about God and evolution, I expounded, with great wisdom, upon the Bible and unfolded hidden mysteries. I knew it all, or so I thought.

In my senior class, I was among a group of students voted most likely to succeed, and one of three voted most witty—actually I spouted biting sarcasm, but my classmates didn't know the difference; they thought I was funny anyway. I was quiet, but everyone knew I had a temper like a grenade and a mouth to go with it. I only had two fights all through school, but I beat the boys so mercilessly that no one dared mess with me after that. What else was I supposed to do? They put their hands under my dress and Granny had told me not to let any boy touch me inappropriately. No one told the teachers about the fights because we would have been expelled from school.

A few times I was caught doing wrong and couldn't finagle my way out of it. One of the times was when our high school got a white physical education teacher for the girls. She wasn't mean or anything, just a prissy straight arrow. I did something silly one day to get her attention. It was out of character for me to do silly things, but sometimes I felt like doing it. I don't remember what I did, but she was livid. She asked me for my home telephone number so she could call Mama. I told her Mama was working. The gym teacher asked for her work number, but I told her Mama was a secretary and couldn't be disturbed. I lied.

Part of me was afraid I would be in serious trouble if she called Mama, and I didn't want to get a whupping for sassing grown folks. Also, I didn't want her to know Mama was a maid. Finally I gave her the number, figuring if Mama answered the phone at the white woman's house, she would talk in her professional voice and the teacher would think it was a business. Everybody knew most black women were maids, but for some reason I didn't want to give the teacher the satisfaction of knowing Mama cleaned houses. I was embarrassed, too. In the end, I don't think she called because Mama never mentioned it to me.

Mama was smart and deserved a better job than cleaning houses, but in the South she had few choices. Granny said Mama was a good student in high school. She was a terrific speller, remembered facts, and added numbers in her head, but she dropped out of school and went to work. Granny was sickly most of her life with a bad heart and high blood pressure and she couldn't work a full-time job. Her husband, Daddy Frank, worked in the fields mostly for whites. He drove their tractors and cultivated the land, earning about 5 dollars a week. With that, he had to pay rent and buy food. They needed extra income so Mama had to work.

Still, Mama was adventurous and loved to travel. As a young woman, she went to New York City to live with Granny's sister, Aunt Ora. Mama found a job and settled in for a long stay, until Granny begged her to come back home because she missed her dearly. When Mama returned, she got married and started having babies, and her world became filled with dirty diapers and hard field work.

Mama said Daddy helped out around the house when they first got married, but as the children got bigger, he stopped. My older siblings learned adult responsibility at a young age because Mama needed help. They looked after the younger children, cleaned, and cooked. My oldest brother Jerry can iron clothes better than I can.

Part II

Fighting a Closed Society

Sit-Ins

In 1958, the Oklahoma City NAACP Youth Council sat at lunch counters and refused to move. There were also sit-ins at a drug store in Kansas. In college towns multiracial groups held sit-ins at restaurants and other segregated public places.

Beginning in 1960, sit-down demonstrations, picket lines, and boycotts spread throughout the South. The most prominent were in Greensboro, North Carolina, where a few black college students organized sit-ins at local stores and the campaign caught on nationwide.

It was inevitable that politics and civil rights would reach a fork in the road. As much as politicians wanted to keep them separate, civil rights were a campaign issue for John Kennedy and Richard Nixon in 1960. For example, Martin Luther King was arrested during a sit-in in Atlanta and he was sentenced to four months of hard labor. The black community was enraged, but Kennedy and Nixon didn't want to intervene and offend white Southerners because they sought their votes. Privately, Kennedy and his staff felt they had to do something. He called King's wife, Coretta Scott King, and asked if there was anything he could do to help. Robert Kennedy then called Atlanta criminal court judge Oscar Mitchell, a Democrat, and asked that King be released. He was released that day from jail.

To show support for Kennedy and his efforts, black ministers around the country endorsed the future president from the pulpit. Although he won over Nixon in a close election, Kennedy did nothing to support blacks' quest for civil rights in the first few months of his presidency, perhaps because he was afraid of upsetting white supporters in the South.

Blacks kept chipping away at the white power structure that had ruled the South and them for centuries. In the midst of breaking down segregation in public schools, blacks next targeted segregated lunch counters at downtown department stores. They wanted to be able to eat at any restaurant they pleased.

The sit-in that made the biggest impact on the civil rights movement occurred on February 1, 1960, in Greensboro, North Carolina. Four black college students directly challenged Southern tradition when they sat down at a lunch counter for whites only and refused to leave. Whites viciously lashed out because they weren't used to blacks sitting with them in restaurants and they weren't about to allow it to happen in their town. They attacked the students, pulling them from the counter stools. The students, who had trained at nonviolent workshops, did not fight back. The sit-ins spread, challenging Jim Crow laws throughout the South.

In Mississippi, Campbell College, which was founded in 1890 in Vicksburg, actively participated in the civil rights movement. The African Methodist Episcopal Church supported the college, which later moved to Jackson in 1898. (It closed in 1964.) Charles A. Jones, the dean of religion at Campbell, led the 1960 Easter boycott of stores in Jackson.

In Nashville, Tennessee, blacks became disgusted because they spent money at white-owned stores downtown but could not sit and eat at department store lunch counters, go to movie theaters, stay at hotels, or ride in the front of city buses.

Some of the students who came from all over the country to attend Nashville's black colleges were not accustomed to the segregated ways of the South, so they decided to do something about it. They planned sit-ins. First they attended workshops during which they were trained in nonviolent tactics, especially how to take mob beatings. U.S. Representative John Lewis, from Georgia, who was a seminary student at the time, was one of the students who took part in the first sit-in.

The well-dressed students marched to the stores and sat there all day doing their homework. Restaurants and lunch counters closed to keep from serving them. For the first two weeks, no one bothered them. Then, groups of bitter white men appeared downtown and assaulted the students. They stomped, kicked, and beat them while police stood by doing nothing.

After the beatings, police arrested more than eighty lunch-counter protesters and charged them with disorderly conduct. The local black community united behind the students and merchants supplied food to those in jails. Homeowners put up property for bail money and a local black lawyer defended the students. The court found the students guilty of disorderly conduct.

John Lewis refused to pay the 50 dollar fine and chose to stay in jail where most of the other students joined him. Parents feared for the safety of their children. Still, blacks were determined to change their way of life and boycotted downtown Nashville stores shortly before the profitable Easter season. As sit-ins spread from the southwest to the southeast, thousands were arrested. A national boycott was organized.

Violence swept through downtown Nashville, where blacks were increasingly being attacked. Whites were afraid to come downtown to shop, go to the movies, or eat at restaurants. The home of Z. Alexander Looby, a black city councilman and lawyer who helped student protesters, was bombed. The blast was so powerful that it shattered the windows in a medical college across the street. No one was killed.

Thousands of blacks joined together, marched downtown, and faced the mayor on the steps of City Hall. They blasted the mayor for not taking a stand against racial injustice in his city. Mayor Ben West responded that he agreed that it was wrong for business owners to sell to blacks but then refuse to provide service to them solely on the basis of their skin color. Weeks later, blacks were served at lunch counters in downtown stores.

After their success in integrating lunch counters, John Lewis and other black college students formed SNCC. Nashville students and others attended an organizing meeting in Raleigh, North Carolina, sponsored by SCLC.

In Mississippi, integration moved at a snail's pace. Whites simply refused to let blacks eat at restaurants with them. The NAACP took action. On May 28, 1963, three Tougaloo students—Anne Moody, Pearlena Lewis, and Memphis Norman—walked through the back door of Woolworth's in Jackson and sat down at the lunch counter.

When they tried to order food, they were told to go to the Negro section. White students from nearby Central High School came in and called the black women every racial epithet they could conjure up. Some customers joined in and for hours they verbally and physically abused the black college students.

Memphis Norman was pulled to the floor, kicked, and beaten. White supporter Joan Trumpauer and white professors Lois Chafee and John Salter from Tougaloo College joined the black students, and the angry whites barraged them, too, with demeaning names. They also poured mustard, catsup, pepper, and water on the demonstrators.

Outside the store, Tougaloo President Daniel Beittel tried to enlist the police to stop the abuse. The store finally closed, and the protesters were jailed. The Jackson sit-ins attracted the attention of Roy Wilkins and other NAACP leaders. Many went to Jackson and joined in the picketing and sit-ins at downtown businesses.

On May 30, 1963, some students at the all-black Lanier High School protested the brutal treatment that the Tougaloo College students suffered at Woolworth's. Around lunchtime, when they walked out of Lanier and gathered in the schoolyard to sing freedom songs, school officials called the police who brought dogs. Students and parents were beaten.

The next day, students from the three black Jackson high schools—Lanier, Jim Hill, and Brinkley—met at Farish Street Baptist Church for nonviolent training. They began marching until police arrested them and jailed them on the Mississippi fairgrounds.

The NAACP, Campbell College's dean of religion Charles A. Jones, and Campbell student body president Alfred Cook, along with people from Jackson State University, Tougaloo College, and the black community in Mississippi, led boycotts of businesses on Capitol Street in Jackson.

They demanded service on a first-come basis. Some of the stores they boycotted were Kent's Dollar Store, H. L. Green's, Wilson Discount Store, and JC Penney's. A Citizens Council official owned Primos Steakhouse, located across the street from the businesses, and the protesters held several sit-ins there as well.

From left to right: Frankye (standing), her brother Jerry, Mama, Daddy, and her sister Martha in Mama's kitchen on Thanksgiving Day in 1975. Author's original family photograph.

Mama and Daddy used to shop at Kent's Dollar Store for our school clothes and supplies, but they stopped for the boycott. They told us stories of blacks who suffered the consequences when they broke the boycott. They were yelled at when they went in the stores, and when they came out with bags, the protesters would grab them and destroy their merchandise. The protesters felt they were working for a cause to benefit everyone and if blacks didn't stick together, the movement would fail.

In the 1970s, Mama shopped at Kent's Dollar Store and sometimes JC Penney's if my oldest sister, who at the time was married and living up North, had sent her some extra money. Mama bought most of her household items and some of our school clothes from Kent's. We only went to Penney's to shop for special occasions, such as Easter. We usually went there on Saturdays when Daddy was off work to drive us. No matter what, all of us got a new outfit for Easter. That's why the boycotts were so significant—because blacks would spend money they didn't have to buy new clothes, especially on a holy day such as Easter. The loss of income from the black community was a huge sum that white business owners couldn't afford to lose.

Equal Treatment

Blacks wanted equal treatment in hiring and promotion, integrated drinking fountains, restrooms, and public transportation, and to be shown respect. The men were fed up with being called "boy" and the women no longer wanted to be called "auntie." Black men wanted to be addressed as Mr. So-and-So and black women preferred Mrs. So-and-So, or Miss So-and-So.

Mama used to tell us about the time a white hobo came to our orange house and asked for some biscuits and water. In those days, hobos often walked around begging for food. She was outside washing clothes when the man walked up and sat on our cistern. "Hey auntie, got any biscuits and water?" the raggedy white man asked. Mama burned inside with rage, but never opened her mouth. When he kept asking her the same question over and over, she turned around and shot back, "I'm not your mother's or father's sister, and neither am I married to anyone in your family, so I ain't your auntie."

Mama knew it was risky talking to a white man like that, but she also knew that well-to-do whites looked down on poor whites. She was just tired of hungry, poor, and homeless whites thinking they were superior to blacks just because of the color of their skin.

Every fragment of Mississippi was divided into a white world and a black world, and for years, no one dared to cross that invisible line, until the 1960s.

The hub of the black community in Jackson was the Farish Street area, which had the Alamo Theater, the Crystal Palace, and black-owned restaurants including Stevens Kitchen, the Home Dining Room, the Big Apple Inn, and Peaches. Across from the Alamo, the "Peanut Man" sold his nuts and Mr. Amos, a blind street vendor, sold sassafras root.

I don't remember eating sassafras root, but Mama and Daddy did buy peanuts from the Peanut Man. They tasted better than

The Alamo Theater, on Farish Street in Jackson, Mississippi, which was under renovation in 2003. Frankye stands beneath the sign. Photo by Marc-Yves Regis I.

any peanuts we ever had. We used to fight over the small bag. Daddy never bought one for each of us; we had to share a bag. We would also stop by the Big Apple Inn, which was a small, hole-in-the-wall restaurant with a jukebox. It's still located on Farish Street and when we visit, my brothers and sisters love going there to buy food. Mama said the original owner was a Mexican who was married to a black woman. They sold Mexican food with a Southern twist.

We usually sat in the car outside while Daddy went inside and brought back our food. The main item was "hot smokes," a small round bun filled with ground smoke sausage and hot sauce that cost a quarter each. At least, that's what it looked and tasted like. Mama said the owners kept the ingredients secret. It was fiery hot. If Mama bought a soda with her food, we all begged her for a sip. "May I have a swallow?" each of us asked. She always got a Coca-Cola in the six-ounce bottle, because she said it tasted better than the larger ones. After we all got our sips, there was nothing left for Mama. When we got home, we had to drink a glass of water to cool down our still-burning tongues.

Sometimes Mama and Daddy got pig-ear sandwiches or hot tamales from the "Hot Tamale Man," but they couldn't afford to go to Stevens Kitchen; it was the so-called upscale restaurant, where civil rights activists met. Volunteers from out of state and leaders like Senator Robert Kennedy, Martin Luther King, Representative Andrew Young, and Vernon Jordan, also met at the restaurant. There were only two hotels where blacks could stay downtown—the Edward Lee Hotel and the Summers Hotel. Although the national YWCA was open to everyone, the facilities at the Jackson headquarters were open only to whites.

Even the Mississippi state fairgrounds sponsored segregated activities for residents. Up until the 1960s, the state held two annual fairs—one for whites and one for blacks. In 1961, the NAACP, its youth councils, and others demonstrated at the "colored" fair. They carried signs that said "No Jim Crow Fair for Us." Police with dogs arrested seven protesters.

In early 1963, Jackson Mayor Allen Thompson said that he would jail up to 10,000 blacks in the fairgrounds' two livestock exhibit buildings, which had been transformed into prisons with hog-wire fences. On May 31, 1963, between 400 and 500 students from age eleven to twenty who attended a mass meeting at Farish Street Baptist Church were arrested and held at the fairgrounds. The students had been at the church to learn about nonviolent protest. When they left the church, they marched down Farish Street toward Capitol Street, where they were loaded by police into city garbage trucks and hauled to the fairgrounds. They crammed the children into the muddy makeshift prison as if they were hogs. Police walked around the place with dogs.

My oldest brother Jerry said that he, too, was jailed at the Mississippi fairgrounds. In the summer of 1968, he joined a student protest on Whitfield Mills Road. Martin Luther King was supposed to have led a "Mule Train," a walking demonstration by poor blacks from Memphis to Washington, D.C., but he was killed that April. So my brother and other students staged their own march to the state

The Mississippi Fairground livestock exhibit building where black youths were jailed in the early 1960s. Frankye's son Marky is standing in front of the building. Photo by Marc-Yves Regis I.

capitol building. Local civil rights leaders told them to maintain a nonviolent posture and keep on walking, even if people threw bricks at them or spit on them. Everything went fine until one of the demonstrators got hit with a rock and fights erupted. The demonstrators attacked whites who had lined the street. They were arrested and housed at the fairgrounds, where my brother said a riot almost broke out when a police officer let his dog attack a pregnant woman.

In the 1960s, many churches participated in the civil rights movement, including Catholic and Episcopal churches. St. Andrew's Episcopal Cathedral in downtown Jackson, which allowed blacks to worship at the church under the leadership of Bishop Duncan M. Gray, Sr., had an interracial "open door" policy.

The Mississippi State Sovereignty Commission spied on the parish and reported on integrated meetings that parish members attended. The commission, which was established in 1956 by the state legislature after the *Brown* decision, was a governmental agency that resembled the racist Citizens Council. The commission had power to subpoena and examine anyone and to demand access to any documents it desired to protect the sovereignty of the state from the federal government.

Frankye's sister Ora and brother Jerry in Milwaukee in July 1971. Author's original family photograph.

The former Pearl Street A.M.E. Church in Jackson was one of twenty local churches that held nightly meetings to support the boycott of downtown businesses. After one meeting in 1963, a list of fair employment and desegregation demands were sent to Mayor Thompson before the sit-ins at Woolworth's department store.

Country Stores

One of the few places where blacks were welcome was whites' country stores. There, blacks could spend their hard-earned money.

As I got older, I began to notice that Granny acted differently around whites, trying her best not to "break verbs"* and speaking properly like the visiting Northerners did. One summer, Granny heard that one of the white families she worked for years ago had

---

* Breaking verbs in Mississippi meant using the wrong verb tense or bad grammar. Blacks in the North called it "busting verbs."

opened a country store, and she wanted to go there and shop. We tried talking her out of going because we knew the merchandise would be overpriced.

Granny usually walked to country stores even though they were several miles from her house. Most people walked in those days. The grocery store chains were located in bigger towns farther away, so the country stores came in handy if we ran out of meal, flour, sugar, or bread, or if we just wanted a snack or something cold to drink. Granny loved Coca-Cola, and sometimes used it as a medicine. When she had a headache, Granny would take two "BC's"—a popular medicinal powder used for headaches and such—and drink a cold Coke. She said it "knocked the headache right out."

Granny wanted to go to the country store because she had spent most of her Social Security check, and she was sure the whites she used to work for would allow her to "take up," or buy some groceries on credit. When we walked into the store, a young white man behind the counter recognized Granny. She used to be his babysitter. He came around the counter and gave her a big hug. Granny called him "Mr. Mark." I felt hot inside. Mark was just a few years older than me and he did not deserve to be called mister, at least not by someone as old as Granny. He called her Bert, without saying "Mrs.," and that angered me even more. The hair on my back stood up, and my head throbbed. I didn't say anything. I knew better than to argue with Granny. You never sassed old folks, especially in public.

They laughed and talked about old times and she reminded him how as a boy, his impishness caused her blood pressure to rise "sky high." They chatted a bit longer before Granny leaned on my arm as we walked around the new store, selecting foods she liked. She noticed that the new store was much bigger than the family's old business. This one looked more like a supermarket, and unlike the old store, this one's food was neatly wrapped in plastic. We got a six-pack of Coca-Cola, some oxtails for soup, a package of lemon cookies, cheese and crackers, souse (hog-headcheese), a jar of pickled pigs' feet, and a loaf of white bread. Granny bought a minimum of healthy stuff. I guess she figured she could eat whatever she wanted because old age and its ailments would probably kill her before food would.

In the old store, Granny said, cookies were stored in a big plastic jar and were sold loose. Pigs' feet were kept in a glass jar and folks used to squeeze their hands through the top and fish around in it until they pulled out the one they wanted. She said people used to come out of the field, dusty and dirty, walk right in that store, and "jook" their grimy hands into a jar of cookies or pig feet. They also broke off hunks of cheese that was sold in ounces or pounds. Souse was also weighed and sold by slices wrapped in waxed paper. The new store didn't have a scale; everything was already weighed and prepackaged with the price stamped on it.

The new country store had no shopping carts; we carried items in our arms and made several trips to the counter. Granny told Mark that she didn't have the money to pay for the stuff right then, but that she would pay him the next month as soon as she got her check in the mail and cashed it. Mark told Granny that the store no longer sold food on credit, but because he had known her since he was a baby, he would let her have a few of the things she had piled on the counter.

I was embarrassed, not for myself but for Granny. I could see the disappointment on her face. Whenever she was disappointed, she would suck her lips in her mouth as though she was trying to ingest them. Her eyes would water a bit and she would become mute. Granny had been so sure Mark would oblige her for all the years she had cared for him and cooked, washed, ironed, and cleaned for his family. Mark fidgeted around with the cash register, pretending to be so absorbed in his work that he didn't see that look on Granny's face.

In her old age, Granny seemed to have forgotten all the things she had taught me about whites. After standing there deciding what to do, she wiped her eyes, forced a nervous smile, and put all the things back except the Coca-Cola, the cheese and crackers, and the oxtails.

When we left the store, I asked Granny why she had called him Mr. Mark. She said, "Baby, when you've been doing things for so long, it becomes natural to you." Granny hadn't even noticed that she called him mister, but I sure did. I wondered if she had called him Mr. Mark when she babysat him, but I didn't ask. I didn't want to know. I wasn't afraid of whites. I had no reason to fear them. Unlike Granny, I hadn't lived through the lynchings, the cross burnings, and the beatings. I had only read about them in books and watched reenactments on television.

Daddy briefly operated a little store when we lived in the orange house. He sold stuff out of a small, red storage house and washroom where we keep the wringer washer, which we had until he bought our first automatic washing machine in 1971. We were his best customers, and all the candy, soda pop, and other junk food we didn't eat, we took to school and gave to our friends. Needless to say, Daddy soon went out of business.

Many blacks refused to talk about Jim Crow laws and how they affected their livelihood. They wanted to "keep it in the past where it belonged, 'cause white folks are good to us now." During rap (discussion) sessions at school with my friends and one of our teachers, we learned about the unspeakable criminal acts some whites had done to blacks. The memories our teacher shared with us had made her loathe white people and those memories burned in my mind like the brand Daddy seared on his cattle. I had never met anyone like her. She hated whites and refused to fear them. She lived her life as if they didn't exist. As much as possible, she stayed away from whites' stores, preferring to support the black-owned hole-in-the-wall businesses. I don't know why I thought of this teacher as I left the country store with Granny that day. Maybe because she had taught me lessons in anger. But Granny, who was older, had lived long enough to learn how to forgive and forget and she knew how to exist with white people. I was still learning.

In the South, from the time we learned to talk, we were trained to address grownups as Mr. and Mrs. So-and-So. When an adult asked us a question, we had to answer "yes, sir," or "yes ma'am," or "no, sir," or "no, ma'am." We didn't have to say "Mr." or "Mrs." to Mama and Daddy, but we did have to say "yes, sir" and "yes, ma'am" to them. If they called us to do something, we couldn't answer with "what?" We had to say "yes, sir" or "yes, ma'am."

As a child, I didn't have a problem addressing older white people as Mr. or Mrs. So-and-So because it was what I had been taught to do. It had nothing to do with their color; they were old, and I was raised to respect old people. But there was no way I was going to say "ma'am" or "sir" to a white person my age or younger, and all the beatings in the world couldn't change the way I felt.

As evil as some whites were to blacks, we couldn't say anything derogatory about them at home. Mama and Daddy didn't allow it because it went against their Christian beliefs. They said people were people, as long as they treated us as human beings. Around my friends, out of earshot of my parents, I said my fair share of "honky," "redneck," "cracker," "peckerwood," and "poor-white trash." These racial slurs sounded silly, but they were all we had. We tried to come up with one that sounded as insulting as the word "nigger," but we couldn't. It was a dumb game because we weren't around whites that much, but we pictured them sitting around all day calling us "niggers" for the heck of it, and if we happened to run into a white racist, we wanted to be prepared to respond.

One Saturday, when I was a teenager, I got my chance when I went with my neighbors to a department store in Clinton. Three of us, all girls, sat in the back seat of a car waiting for one girl's mother to come out of the store. Through the back window, we noticed a couple of young white boys hunched behind the car we sat in. We got out and chased them, but they ran away laughing. When we walked back to the car and inspected the area where they had been, we saw the word NIGGERS written in the dust on the car with their fingers. We were so furious, we started shouting all the racial slurs we could think of. We had no idea what they meant, but it made us feel good to say them.

When I got home, I asked Granny what "redneck" means. She said it was coined from whites who worked outside in construction. It was so hot in Mississippi that their necks turned red. "Cracker" came from the "soda cracker," she said, the color of which supposedly matched white people's skin. "Peckerwood" described whites' long, pointed noses, like a woodpecker's bill. Granny didn't know where "honky" came from, and "poor white trash" spoke for itself. This was probably the most stinging slur of all because whites didn't think they were supposed to be poor and dirty.

White people thought poverty was reserved for blacks, but Mississippi had its share of poor whites, and they were the ones who gave us the most trouble. I suppose it was economics—we competed for the same jobs as them, especially after the civil rights movement when young blacks, freshly armed with civil and voting rights, finally had a voice. A new generation of young black militants emerged in the seventies and they weren't about to let whites treat them like dogs. A popular saying was, "You can kick a dog for so long until it gets up and bites you in the butt."

My brothers and sisters and I respected Dr. Martin Luther King and his legacy, and we appreciated all he had done for blacks, but we were not fans of his nonviolent approach to exercising our natural rights as human beings. We wanted what any other law-abiding citizen of the United States wanted—a proper education, a well-paying job after college, and a safe neighborhood to live in. We believed we were entitled to these things without allowing whites to spit on us, clobber our heads, or kill us just because we were born black. We didn't promote violence and we didn't go looking for trouble, but if a white person were to attack us, we vowed to defend ourselves to the death.

One time Mama heard us discussing this and she shook her head. "I'm so glad none of y'all was born during slavery because all of y'all would've been killed," she said.

Doctors

There were few doctors who treated blacks, but when Mama had asthma attacks and could barely breathe, a white doctor from Clinton would make house calls. That doctor had an office in Clinton and in the 1970s, blacks were welcome there. They sat in the same waiting room as whites. There was another white doctor down the street who had two entrances, one for blacks and one for whites. I didn't know about the separate doors until I was a teenager, after they were painted over, but people still went to their respective rooms. It had been that way for so long that it was normal for them.

The dentist office had been segregated too. I never knew blacks had a separate waiting room because it wasn't unusual to go somewhere and find a group of blacks together. I didn't figure it out until the day I went to the dentist alone and walked in the wrong door. There wasn't a sign that said "Whites Only" and I didn't know I was supposed to know the difference. I noticed whites staring at me, but I had no idea why. No one said anything and neither did I.

I hated going to the dentist. Not because the office was segregated, but because the dentist was a monster. He never consulted with me, never tried to save my teeth. If I went there with a toothache, he yanked out the tooth. It was horrible. He would poke a long needle filled with Novocain into my gums around the aching tooth. Then he took this pliers-like instrument and grabbed the tooth, leaning his fat self heavily against my body. I heard the cracking noise the tooth made as this madman struggled to pull it out. I grabbed both arms of the chair and slid my bottom from side to side. I wanted to slap him.

"You don't feel the pain, it's just the pressure," that idiot would say. We begged Mama and Daddy not to take us back to him, but he was the cheapest dentist around. Five dollars a tooth. Our parents didn't know any better and when we had a toothache, Daddy immediately said it needed to be pulled. When I got older, I stopped telling them if I had toothaches. At night, when the pain was unbearable, I would take two aspirins and wrap a towel around a hot iron and hold it to my face until the warmth eased the pain in my teeth and gums. God was surely watching over us because sometimes we cried ourselves to sleep, but the iron never burned our faces.

Black people had a medicine for every ailment. When Mama had migraines and no money to go to the doctor, Granny would go into the pasture, get some leaves—I don't know what kind of tree she got them from—put them on Mama's forehead, and then wrap a white cloth bandage around her head. Granny did the same thing for us when we had headaches.

When we had stomachaches, Mama gave us "as-fiz-dy."* We never pronounced it correctly because Southerners tend to drops letters

---

* The correct word is asafetida, which is a gum resin from Asiatic plants of the parsley family. It was formerly used in folk medicine to treat some illnesses.

and slur words because of our drawl. (We blame the blazing sun, which zaps our energy, resulting in lazy tongues. Granny used to say that it was too hot to talk.) Mama and Daddy bought as-fiz-dy in chunks from the drugstore. When they squeezed it into a small bottle and added water, the concoction smelled like garlic and vinegar mixed together. A tablespoon of that stuff took care of a bellyache.

In my teen years, however, I had a stomachache that as-fiz-dy didn't cure. Mama took me to the doctor in Clinton, and he put me on a bland diet and told Mama not to let me eat fried foods, milk products—especially chocolate milk—and caffeine. How could I not eat fried foods in the South? Mama fried everything—chicken, corn, potatoes, and fish—but she started baking all of my meats and draining grease from my vegetables. Still, the pain continued.

Mama took me back to the doctor in Clinton and he referred her to a gastroenterologist in Jackson. The specialist was nothing like our regular doctor, who was not afraid to touch a black person. Mama said that when he first opened his practice in Clinton, he spoke with an accent. She didn't know what country he emigrated from, but she said blacks kept him in business.

The specialist never examined me or ran any tests. He just looked at me and said I would have to suffer with my stomach problems for the rest of my life. He wouldn't touch me, but he sure took Mama's money.

I was leery of doctors after that and didn't trust them. One time I hurt my knee and Mama took me to another doctor in Clinton. Our regular doctor had retired. The new doctor examined my leg and told me that in the next few years I could come back and he would tie my Fallopian tubes to prevent me from getting pregnant. I was taken aback because I was there for my knee, not my reproduction organs. I told him no. Tie my tubes! I wasn't even sexually active. Why would I want my tubes tied? He never asked me about my sex life, and he didn't explain why he wanted to tie my tubes, especially since I didn't ask him to. All I could think of was that he wanted to stop me from having babies, more black babies, like the eight Mama had.

Mama only took us to the doctor for serious stuff. We didn't go for every little pain we had. When I played in a wasp nest and they stung me, Granny pulled down her bottom lip, dug out some snuff with her forefinger, and pasted it on the sting. If I had an allergic reaction to bee stings, I never knew it because the snuff eased the pain and stopped the swelling.

Granny also pasted my body with snuff one time when I fell into a fire ant pile. Mama was picking cotton in the field behind the orange house and Granny was babysitting my younger brothers and me. I told Granny that I was going to see Mama in the field. When I got there, I decided to hide and called out to Mama to find me. Mama begged me to come to her, but I lay down between two rows of cotton. "Come here baby," she pleaded. But I said, "No, find me." Suddenly, I felt bites all over my body. Mama ran to me and stripped off my clothes. Granny heard me screaming and ran down to the field. When she saw the blisters all over my body, she dipped her finger in

Frankye's brother Paul, Frankye, and her brother Robert in their living room in 1980. Author's original family photograph.

her bottom lip and dug out a pile of snuff, which she smeared all over me. I guess it worked because I don't have any scars.

Every old person I knew in Mississippi dipped snuff or chewed tobacco. Granny loved snuff, and she would pack it in her bottom lip and spit it out when it became watery so that she wouldn't swallow it. Granny carried her snuffbox everywhere she went, along with her spit cup, which was an empty coffee can. At home, she placed her spit cup under the bed. Children would be slapped "up side" the head for accidentally knocking over a spit cup. Tobacco products didn't have the stigma then that they have today. You never heard of anyone dying of cancer from tobacco. People were more likely to die from something else.

In the rural South, death always seemed near. I remember the time my two youngest brothers, Paul and Robert, and I were playing with a neighbor in the backyard at the orange house. When we got hungry, we asked our neighbor, because he was older and bigger than we were, to climb the persimmon tree in our backyard and shake it so that we could eat some of its gooey fruit. After he shook the tree hard, I felt something run down my face. I thought some mushy persimmons had fallen on my head. My brothers ran over to inspect my head and saw a gaping wound. The stick our neighbor had used to beat the tree limbs had fallen from his hands and struck me. I thought I was going to die. He begged me not to tell Mama and Daddy about what happened. It was an accident and I didn't tell.

Robert and Paul carried me to Mama and she shaved off my hair, washed the cut, and poured alcohol on my head so that the cut wouldn't get infected. She ripped up a white sheet and used a piece of it to bandage my head. I don't know what we told Mama happened that day, but it must have satisfied her because she didn't get mad.

I still have that scar on my head.

Freedom Summer

During the summer of 1964, Mississippi found itself thrust into the public eye. Civil rights volunteers spread across the state and risked being beaten or killed to open the "closed society." It was called Freedom Summer. The Council of Federated Organizations (COFO) was the overseer, and SNCC and CORE organized a statewide voter registration drive.

In communities, COFO engaged in direct action campaigns and provided statewide organizational support. Like other segregationists, white Mississippians had fought with a vengeance to keep their lives separate from blacks. In 1954, the Citizens Council was established in the Mississippi Delta, where blacks outnumbered whites, to preserve white political power by fighting against integration. Chapters spread across the state and ruled it until 1963.

Bankers, politicians, and business owners joined Citizen Council chapters throughout the South. They punished people who supported integration or black voting rights by foreclosing mortgages, denying loans to farmers, or firing workers. They also used their influence to push through laws to ensure white dominance.

Blacks' votes were significant because in some counties they outnumbered whites. But in many counties no blacks were registered to vote because they would lose their jobs if they did so. Blacks were threatened, put in jail, or thrown off plantations for attempting to vote. Some were murdered. The state passed new voting laws to make registration even more difficult.

Meanwhile, tension was building in Jackson, where NAACP State Field Secretary Medgar Evers was leading protestors. His wife Myrlie served as his secretary. For more than a decade, Evers had fought for racial justice. In 1963, he led the first attempt to integrate First Baptist Church. But integration would take ten more years before the Reverand R.L.T. Smith and the Reverand Emmet

Burns became the first blacks to worship there. In 1976, Lawrence Manguary became the first black member.

Evers had also helped organize the NAACP boycott of Jackson's stores in 1963. He urged blacks not to shop on Capitol Street. He wanted merchants to feel the economic pinch. The stores, Evers said, helped support the white Citizens Council, which wanted to keep blacks down as second-class citizens.

In downtown Jackson, demonstrators were beaten. Students left their schools to protest the abuse and hundreds were arrested. On June 11, 1963, President Kennedy made a speech on civil rights. "A great change is at hand and the task or obligation is to make it peaceful and constructive for everyone," he said. "Those who do nothing invite shame and violence. Those who act boldly recognize right and reality."

That night, returning home from a meeting at New Jerusalem Baptist Church, Evers was murdered in his own driveway. He was shot in the back. He was taken to the University of Mississippi Medical Center where he died. His personal doctor stood and watched because black doctors were not allowed to operate in the segregated emergency room. A fingerprint found at the scene matched that of Byron De La Beckwith, a member of the Citizen Council in Greenwood, Mississippi. He was tried twice but both of the all-white juries were hung and he was set free.

Evers' funeral was held at the Masonic Temple on Lunch Street in Jackson. Fourteen hundred mourners marched from the temple to Collins Funeral Home, which was one of two funeral homes on Farish Street in downtown Jackson. The ninety-minute service was attended by NAACP Executive Secretary Roy Wilkins, United Nations Assistant Secretary General Ralph Bunche, and Martin Luther King. Evers was buried in Arlington Cemetery in Virginia with full military honors.

Collins Funeral Home also handled my grandmother's funeral. Every black person I knew called Collins or People's Funeral Home when someone in his or her family died. Because of segregation, blacks and whites could not use the same funeral homes.

After Evers' funeral, a crowd of mourners began walking toward downtown, singing freedom songs. When they reached Capitol

Medgar Evers' house in 2003 and the driveway where he was assassinated. Photo by Marc-Yves Regis I.

Street, police with billy clubs and police dogs were waiting. Some marchers threw bricks, bottles, rocks, and other things. Some of the protesters were arrested.

Civil rights leaders and sympathetic whites traveled to Mississippi to see firsthand what was going on. They, too, were met with brutal resistance. Police followed them around and beat them, charging them with made-up crimes. They were threatened and told to leave Mississippi.

In June 1964, Robert Moses of SNCC announced Freedom Summer. He hoped to send up to 1,000 teachers, ministers, lawyers, and students from all over the country to Mississippi to establish Freedom Schools and community center programs, and to conduct voter registration activities and research. He hoped volunteers would work in white communities and push through a program designed to open up Mississippi to the rest of the country.

State officials were not pleased. Mississippi Governor Paul Johnson called in more highway patrols and the city of Jackson brought in armored trucks to stop student volunteers from going there. When Lieutenant Governor Paul Johnson had run for governor of Mississippi in 1963, I memorized his campaign song, which constantly played on the radio. It went like this: "Paul B. Johnson, Paul B. Johnson, Paul B. Johnson is your man!" I guess I remember it because at the time, I had a baby brother named Paul.

The volunteers, who were mostly students from large universities and came from middle- and upper-class families, trained in Oxford, Ohio. The white students were used to portray angry white mobs. They beat each other up and practiced calling each other niggers and nigger lovers. They were warned that there would be violence and that some people would die.

The first recruits included Andrew Goodman, twenty, a student from New York City who left on June 20, 1964, for Mississippi. Goodman joined CORE worker James Chaney, twenty-one, and Michael Schwerner, twenty-four, a New York social worker. On June 21, the three civil rights workers went to investigate the burning of a black Methodist church, where a civil rights meeting had been held weeks before. A Freedom School was supposed to be opened at the church. That afternoon, a Sheriff's deputy stopped their car outside of Philadelphia, Mississippi. They were arrested and then released from a Neshoba County jail that night, but the deputy sheriff and Klan members stopped the car again, took the three men to an isolated area, and shot them to death.

The disappearance of Goodman, Chaney, and Schwerner made national news and President Lyndon Johnson, who became president after Kennedy's assassination, ordered a massive search. FBI agents and Mississippi sailors from Meridian joined in the search. It was widely believed that if Chaney, the black civil rights worker, had been alone that night, the disappearance would have gone overlooked like so many others. But the fact that two young white students were with him gave the case prominence. President Johnson met with the mothers of Schwerner and Goodman and sent FBI Director J. Edgar Hoover to Mississippi to set up an FBI office in Jackson.

By late July the three civil rights workers had been missing for six weeks and many lost hope that they would ever be found alive. On August 4, 1964, an informant led the FBI to a farm outside of

Philadelphia, where the three bodies were found buried together in an earthen dam. The men had been shot with .38 caliber bullets. Cheney, the black victim, had suffered severe bone and skull fractures.

On August 7, 1964, James Cheney was buried in Meridian, Mississippi. His parents and those of Michael Schwerner wanted their sons buried side-by-side in Meridian, but Mississippi law forbade integration even in cemeteries.

The state of Mississippi did not bring charges, but the federal government charged nineteen men with conspiracy to deprive the men of their civil rights. In 1967, seven, including the deputy sheriff, were convicted and sentenced to prison terms ranging from three to ten years. Three were acquitted and three were set free by a hanged jury.

Despite the danger, volunteers poured into Mississippi. Many were beaten and thousands were arrested. They went to rural areas, trying to build support for a new political party. The Mississippi Freedom Democratic Party (MFDP) was organized and people, black and white, were invited to join. COFO coordinated the challenge to the all-white Mississippi delegation to the national Democratic Party's August 1964 convention in Atlantic City, New Jersey. Police harassed the volunteers by ticketing, arresting, and jailing them.

The volunteers held a "Freedom Registration Drive" throughout the state. Precinct meetings and district caucuses were held, and on August 6, in Jackson, COFO held a state convention. They elected a slate of delegates for the national convention and asked to be seated as the only Democratic constitutional body of Mississippi. Sixty thousand people risked their lives and signed up.

Although President Johnson signed the Civil Rights Act in July 1964, it did not give blacks the right to vote. The new law, however, gave the federal government more power to ban discrimination in public places.

For years most blacks had been denied a decent education in Mississippi. SNCC opened forty-one Freedom Schools throughout the state. During the day, the volunteers taught reading, writing, math, and black history. At night, the schools were used for political meetings where the new political party was discussed and new members were signed up.

The white volunteers offended many white Mississippians because the volunteers taught in black schools and lived in blacks' homes, proving that blacks and whites could live and work together.

In August 1964, the state's Democratic Party met to select delegates to the National Convention. Blacks were not allowed to participate because the Democratic Party, too, discriminated against them. The MFDP held its own convention and chose its own delegates to challenge the all-white Democratic slate of delegates to represent the state. For many, it was their first trip out of Mississippi. The delegation of sixty-four blacks and four whites left for Atlantic City.

The MFDP delegates wanted to be seated at the National Convention as representatives of their home state, but the Johnson administration had other plans. Johnson anticipated no opposition to getting his party's nomination and he was concerned that the MFDP would disrupt party unity.

At the Convention, the Democratic Party had to decide which of the two delegations from Mississippi would represent the state on the floor. The credentials committee had to choose. On Saturday, August 27, America watched this nationally televised hearing.

Mrs. Fannie Lou Hamer, a sharecropper from Ruleville, Mississippi, spoke at the hearing. She said that if the MFDP wasn't "seated now, I question America. Is this America? The land of the free and the home of the brave? Where we have to sleep with our telephones off of the hook, because our lives be threatened daily because we want to live as decent human beings in America."

During her testimony, in which she described being brutally beaten when she tried to vote, Johnson called a press conference and effectively cut off coverage of the network broadcast by asking for network air time. He did not want the MFDP party seated because he was afraid Southerners would desert the Democratic Party if this happened. He pressured liberals close to the freedom Democrats.

Minnesota Senator Hubert Humphrey, who many believed would not be selected as vice president if he did not help stop the MFDP, assigned Walter Mondale, his young protégé from Minnesota, to work out a deal to satisfy everyone. The first offer was for MFDP to come to the convention and speak out but not vote.

MFDP rejected it. The second offer was to give MFDP two seats at large, which meant they would not represent the state of Mississippi. It would allow the all-white Democrats to be seated while the at-large delegates would be guests. In addition, at the next convention in 1968, the Democratic Party would refuse to seat any state delegation that discriminated against blacks. Another suggestion was that everyone would be seated if they pledged loyalty to the Democratic Party. MFDP's attorney and other black leaders outside of Mississippi pressured the group to accept the compromise, but MFDP refused to accept the two-seat plan, although the convention approved it.

The agreement didn't please everyone. All but four of the regular white delegates from Mississippi walked out of the convention. National civil rights leaders urged the MFDP to accept the compromise, but they voted overwhelmingly to turn it down. Fannie Lou Hamer, vice chairperson of the MFDP, said, "We didn't come all this way for no two seats when all of us is tired."

The MFDP delegates made one last appeal. They tried to sit in the seats abandoned by the regular Mississippi delegates. They were not seated. They returned to Mississippi with a loss of faith in America's leaders. But their protests were the key to opening up the Democratic Party and changing national politics. During the legislature's 1965 special summer session, MFDP held three weeks of demonstrations at the Capitol, demanding electoral reform. Police arrested more than 600 demonstrators.

Johnson announced that Humphrey would be his running mate. Johnson had also signed the Civil Rights Act of 1964 that Kennedy had sent to Congress. The act, among other things, gave the Justice Department power to sue to integrate public facilities and schools. The Equal Employment Opportunity Commission (EEOC) was created along with rules to ban discrimination in hiring.

On December 10, 1964, Martin Luther King won the Nobel Peace Prize. Despite this honor, J. Edgar Hoover continued his efforts to destroy King. Hoover was in charge of COINTELPRO, a secret and illegal FBI operation that spied on citizens. The code name COINTELPRO was an acronym for a series of FBI domestic counterintelligence programs from 1956 to 1971, designed to stop anyone whom the government considered an enemy.

Civil rights leaders, including King, the Black Panthers, and the Communist Party, were targets. The covert operations were illegal because agents discredited constitutionally protected political activity. Some of the tactics they used were infiltrating targeted organizations, threatening black leaders, giving the media false information, sending anonymous letters, and making anonymous telephone calls. They also had people arrested on false charges, and conducted break-ins, assaults, and beatings.

This was the same government that supposedly was trying to help blacks gain their civil rights. When I watched the Hollywood-made movie *Mississippi Burning*, I laughed at how FBI agents were portrayed as sympathetic to blacks. This was not the case. Most blacks did not trust them because they were white men who carried guns and held the same racist views as the Southern lawmakers who were murdering blacks.

Struggle

ccratic Convention, black ac-
cemocrats in Mississippi and
in Selma, Alabama, SNCC
and faced stiff resistance. In
January, Selma's black leaders turned to Martin Luther King and
the SCLC for help.

Dallas County Courthouse in Alabama was the site of mass
protests to win voter rights legislation. More than half the population of Dallas County was black and few were registered voters. In
Selma, the registrar's office was opened only two days a week.

President Johnson proposed eliminating voting rights obstacles to
blacks, but Dallas County Sheriff Jim Clark had his own idea about
who should vote in Alabama. He personally showed up on the courthouse steps and hit blacks with his billy club if they tried to register
to vote. Some protesters were killed. His men used electric cattle
prods against blacks who demonstrated or tried to vote.

King arrived in Selma in early 1965 to help blacks to the courthouse to register. More than 200 blacks were arrested for unlawful
assembly. King was also arrested and spent four days in jail. A federal district judge issued an order prohibiting Clark and his men
from keeping blacks from registering. Blacks in surrounding Alabama towns came out in droves to protest and state troopers went
on the attack, shooting and killing demonstrator Jimmy Lee Jackson. When King spoke at his memorial service, he criticized the
federal government for conducting the war in Vietnam when blacks
were being denied equal rights in their own country. Thousands of
blacks were arrested, even peaceful demonstrators.

In response to the killings of civil rights workers, SCLC organized a fifty mile march from Selma to Montgomery. Governor Wallace was determined that the march would not take place. On

March 7, 1965, hundreds of people gathered at Brown Chapel AME Church to march anyway. That day, King was not in Selma, and SNCC members did not participate.*

Police were nowhere to be found. The marchers crossed the Edmund Pettus Bridge into Montgomery. Waiting on the other side were Alabama state troopers. Wallace ordered them to stop the marchers. Police in riot gear beat them back and shot tear gas. Police officers on horses chased the people.

"Bloody Sunday" was broadcast nationally and people from all over the country came to Selma to support the demonstrators. More than 400 white clergy came also. One of them, the Reverand James Reeb, a Unitarian from Boston, was attacked and killed. Vice President Humphrey attended his funeral. President Johnson called Reeb's wife. Some blacks were offended because Jimmy Lee Jackson's family did not get the same treatment when he was murdered in Alabama.

A few days later, a second march was scheduled and a district judge issued a restraining order for the march. King defied the federal order and led demonstrators to Montgomery until they reached the bridge, where authorities were again waiting. This time, thousands of marchers, including politicians, labor and church leaders, SNCC members, and some Southern whites, participated. A judge blocked the march and when the marchers reached the bridge, police asked them to stop. The marchers asked if they could kneel and pray and permission was granted. Then King had everyone turn around and walk back across the bridge. SNCC leaders were angry with King for turning back.

Later in Washington, President Johnson met with Governor Wallace, who still refused to provide police protection for the marchers. A few days later, Johnson addressed Congress, asking for a comprehensive voting rights bill. "Their cause must be our cause, too; it's not just Negroes, but really it's all of us who must overcome the crippling legacy of bigotry and injustice, and we shall overcome."

---

* SNCC's head office resented it when King's workers appeared at high-profile demonstrations after SNCC workers had risked their lives to start a campaign. SNCC's regional leaders eventually joined the march.

The judge eventually lifted the injunction and allowed the march to proceed, but Wallace still refused to protect the marchers. President Johnson federalized the Alabama National Guard and on March 21, 1965, more than two months after the first march was attempted, thousands gathered at Brown Chapel Church for a march to Montgomery. The Alabama National Guard checked for bombs and prepared to protect the marchers.

"We're going to walk nonviolently and peacefully," said King. "Let the nation and the world know we are tired now. We've lived with slavery and segregation 345 years; we've waited a long time for freedom. We're trying to remind the nation of the urgency of the moment, now is the time to make real the promises of democracy. Now is the time to transform Alabama, the heart of Dixie, to a state with a heart for brotherhood, and peace and goodwill. Now is the time to make justice a reality for all of God's children."

SCLC invited people from all over the country to participate in the Sunday march on March 21. It ended on March 25 with more than 25,000 people participating.

On the way to Montgomery, the SCLC heard about a plot against King's life, but he refused to turn back. That night the KKK murdered a white housewife as she drove marchers back to Selma. Viola Gregg Liuzzo, a Michigan mother of five, had come to Selma to participate in the march. Four men were arrested and three were indicted in an Alabama court. The first trial ended in a hung jury. The second one, with an all-white jury, found the men not guilty. The Justice Department stepped in and charged the men with violating Liuzzo's civil rights. A federal jury found them guilty and the judge sentenced them to ten years in prison.

On August 6, 1965, President Johnson signed the Voting Rights Act of 1965 into law. No longer could Southern white racists keep blacks from registering to vote by giving them literacy tests. And in the Deep South, which had openly discriminated against blacks who attempted to register, federal registrars could administer the registrations. Black registration increased. On paper, blacks had civil and voting rights. But, you cannot regulate the hearts and minds of people. The struggle was not over, but a new phase of militant blacks had sprung up.

Five days later the Watts section of Los Angeles exploded in violence. Thousands were injured and more than thirty people died. The six-day riot began after a white state highway patrol officer stopped a young black man for erratic driving and arrested him. A crowd surrounded them and a fight broke out. Thousands of people were arrested. During the Watts riots, white-owned stores were looted and burned.

Blacks also rioted in Tuskegee, Alabama. SNCC was conducting a voter registration campaign when a white man killed an SNCC worker who tried to use a bathroom reserved for whites at a gas station.

By the time the voting rights bill became law, SNCC was in Lowndes County, Alabama, fighting for voting rights.

On August 20, 1965, after arrests at a demonstration, a white man shot and killed Jonathan Daniels, a white Episcopal seminary student from New Hampshire, and wounded a Catholic priest from Chicago. An all-white jury acquitted him of manslaughter.

In 1966, Klan members burned numerous crosses on blacks' property to frighten them. Klan members also murdered outspoken leader, Vernon Dahmer, a black grocer from Hattiesburg who supported the volunteer voter registration workers. Klan leader Sam Bowers was later convicted for the murder.

Despite the violence, things slowly began to change in the South. As part of the federal government's war on poverty, the Office of Economic Opportunity distributed funds to the Child Development Group of Mississippi to operate centers that educated young children from poor families. The federal Head Start program grew out of the Mississippi program.

In June 1966, James Meredith, who integrated Ole Miss, led the March Against Fear, a 220-mile pilgrimage through Mississippi to encourage blacks to register to vote. A white man in ambush shot Meredith, who was not seriously injured, on a highway. Meredith said he had asked for federal protection but did not receive it. When the march resumed, both King and SNCC, led by Stokely Carmichael, took part in it. At the Capitol in Jackson on June 26, 1966, Meredith, Martin Luther King, NAACP field secretary

Charles Evers (Medgar Evers' brother), and NAACP State Chairman Aaron Henry spoke to a crowd of about 20,000 spectators.

Meanwhile, in Lowndes County in Alabama, after federal registrars went there and registered blacks, the Democratic Party would not allow black candidates to run in its primaries. The blacks formed their own party called the Black Panther Party, with a Black Power symbol. CORE followed the lead of SNCC, which had already begun to lean toward becoming an all-black organization with only black leaders. Bob and Dorothy Miller Zellner had worked for SNCC for years; Bob Zellner was its first white field secretary. But SNCC members felt that whites should organize their own communities. Black pride was making a comeback and blacks wanted to be in charge of their own organizations.

Although Martin Luther King continued to preach nonviolence, times were changing. On April 4, 1968, as King stood on the balcony of the Lorraine Hotel in Memphis, he was shot and killed. He was in

The Lorraine Motel where Martin Luther King was murdered. Photo by Marc-Yves Regis I, September 1997.

Memphis to help city garbage collectors demonstrate for better working conditions. Mama cried that day we heard it on the radio. She was washing dishes or cooking and I was playing in the backyard. I was nine years old and I cried too; I don't know why. I cried because Mama was crying. I thought that man King was a friend of Mama's. Maybe she thought her dream of freedom died with King.

James Earl Ray was convicted for the shooting and sentenced to ninety-nine years in prison, where he died in 1998. He was a high-school dropout and small-time criminal who many believed was not smart enough to plan a major assassination alone. Shortly before he died, Ray insisted that he did not kill King, whose family believed the murder had been part of a conspiracy and pushed to reopen the case.

Growing up, I heard that King's murder was ordered by some man named Hoover. I didn't know who Hoover was, or what the FBI or the federal government were for that matter. But as a child, I was not allowed to ask many questions. Children had to believe what they were told.

Part III

The Price of Freedom

Black Nationalism and Black Power

Many people believe that the civil rights movement died with Martin Luther King. But where King left off, the militant black movement took over. Young blacks were no longer willing to overcome racial oppression through nonviolence. No one was reigning in the racist whites who brutalized innocent blacks demonstrating peacefully for equal rights. Why should blacks cover themselves with their arms and fall down in fetal positions so that whites could beat them into unconsciousness?

In the mid-1960s, instead of singing "We Shall Overcome Someday," young blacks were raising their fists and shouting "Black Power." But before Black Power, there was Black Nationalism in 1963. Blacks began to think that maybe integration was not the answer. Maybe blacks could create their own states and separate from the white race altogether. What was the difference? There was already de facto segregation. In the North and in large cities, blacks were just as separated and unequal as they were in the South.

Unlike blacks in the South, however, urban blacks in the North started revolting against white oppression, especially when it came to brutality involving white police officers. There were many cases in which a white police officer shot an unarmed black person "in the line of duty" and was then cleared of all charges. These scenarios smacked of the same racism that occurred in the Deep South, where white racist Sheriff deputies mutilated and murdered black people, particularly black men, and all-white juries acquitted them.

The same crime still happens today. In 1997 in New Milford, Connecticut, white police officer Scott Smith shot and killed Franklyn Reid. Smith was convicted of manslaughter but the conviction was overturned. Also in Connecticut in 1997, Robert Flodquist, a New Haven police officer, fatally shot Malik Jones after a high-speed chase. The officer had ordered him out of his car. When Jones started backing up his car, Flodquist opened fire. He was cleared of any criminal wrongdoing.

In April 1999, white officer Robert Allan shot and killed fourteen-year-old Aquan Salmon, who was a suspect in an attempted street robbery. The youth carried a cigarette lighter that looked like a gun. The officer was cleared of shooting the teenager in the back as he fled. In February 1999, four New York City police officers shot forty-one bullets into an unarmed West African immigrant named Amadou Diallo. They were acquitted. Singer Bruce Springsteen later wrote about the incident in a song. These are just a few of the numerous cases in modern times of police brutality against unarmed blacks.

During the civil rights movement, only a few cases like this were high profile and many nameless black men and women were murdered. The backlash started sporadically with race riots in Detroit in 1943 and then heated up again in 1964 in New York City, Rochester, New York, and Philadelphia. Violence escalated with the Watts uprising in 1965 when a California highway patrol officer pulled over a drunk driver in Watts, a section of South Los Angeles. A six-day riot ensued, with violence, looting, and burning of buildings. Thirty-four people died and thousands were arrested.

These riots revealed another kind of segregation and discrimination—outside of the South—particularly in housing. During the Great Migration from the South, millions of blacks left rural areas and crowded into ghettos. While growing up, I remember hearing Granny say that to flee oppression in Mississippi, all a black person had to do was cross the invisible Mason-Dixon Line, which divided the North from the South. During many summers when we took the train to Milwaukee to visit my older brother and sisters and it crossed into Missouri, Granny would say that we were free.

The migration started during World War II when blacks filled factory jobs vacated by white men who went off to war. But blacks found themselves segregated in crowded public housing. They had fled the slavery of Jim Crow and ended up imprisoned by the trappings of government assistance, which kept them economically enslaved for generation after generation.

In Northern neighborhoods where black people moved, whites fled to newly built suburbs and built their own schools and businesses. Real estate agents were also guilty of "redlining" and steering blacks to all-black neighborhoods. In the 1960s and 1970s, banks and mortgage lenders typically singled out a black neighborhood and denied its occupants loans to buy homes. The symbolic red line around minority neighborhoods meant that mortgage loan applications were discouraged or denied. The results were higher mortgages for blacks and less competition for homes. The Fair Housing Act, which Congress passed in 1968, was supposed to rectify housing discrimination in sales, rentals, and lending, but discriminatory practices lasted for years.

In the South, blacks and whites lived side-by-side on the same property because of sharecropping but did not socialize with each other. In the South, the big differences in living conditions told the whole story. Whites lived in mansions and blacks lived in shacks. Because of slavery and then sharecropping, blacks lived in every city, town, or rural area of Mississippi. Blacks were allowed to live nearby because whites needed them to cook, clean, babysit, and do other domestic chores.

In the North, however, whites didn't want blacks living near them and fought housing integration with a vengeance. National Guardsmen were sent to Cicero, Illinois, when blacks moved into the town in 1952 and whites rioted and chased them out.

In 1966, King and the SCLC took their nonviolent campaign up North to fight housing discrimination. Demonstrations in all-white Chicago neighborhoods evoked riots because whites were not ready for forced integration. Although city officials promised changes, nothing substantial occurred. Direct action, which had proven successful in the South, failed to tear down racist practices in the North.

Black Nationalism had been on the rise before the death of nonviolent protest, which was staunchly criticized by Nation of Islam leader Malcolm X, who promoted self-defense "by any means necessary." The Nation of Islam was founded in 1930. I remember listening to the radio on Saturdays in the early 1970s and hearing the voice of the Honorable Elijah Muhammad, the group's leader at the time, talk about the evils of blue-eyed devils. I had never heard a black man talk about white people like that before. A black man in Mississippi would be hanged for saying the things

Muhammad was saying. And yet, there was nothing whites could do to him. The Nation of Islam was up North and out of the reach of racist white Southerners.

I also remember hearing Nation of Islam leaders preach about black self-sufficiency and Black Pride. I assume there was a temple in Mississippi at the time, but we never went. We were not Muslims; we were National Baptists and attended the church down the road every Sunday. But at the time it didn't seem strange to me that Mama and Daddy listened to that radio program. Muhammad talked about racial pride and hard work, and Mama and Daddy could identify with these things because they worked hard in the fields and at home to provide a better life for us. Nation of Islam leaders said things we had never heard before and, although we were not followers, their words were uplifting.

Malcolm X was the most charismatic member of the Nation of Islam. He was a spokesperson, recruiter, temple organizer, and fundraiser. Born Malcolm Little in 1925 in Omaha, Nebraska, he served time in prison for burglary. It was there that he became a Muslim and changed his last name, which he considered a slave name. Malcolm X was thirty-nine years old when Nation of Islam gunmen killed him in 1965 as he delivered a speech in a New York City ballroom. A rift had developed between Elijah Muhammad and the more articulate Malcolm, who had gained widespread recognition because of his powerful speeches. The rift became so great that Malcolm eventually split from the Nation of Islam and formed his own organization, the Organization of Afro-American Unity. But Malcolm's devotion to Black Pride left a mark on blacks in the North and South. Black Nationalism evolved into Black Power.

Young, black civil rights leaders in the South also began spouting Black Power. SNCC members decided that they no longer wanted to practice nonviolence to gain equal rights. During James Meredith's March Against Fear through Mississippi in 1966, SNCC chairman Stokely Carmichael began using the phrase "Black Power."

I went around raising my fist and saying "Black Power," which made me feel proud and powerful. I felt like I was on top of the world and that no white person could tell me what to do, scare me, or boss me around. Blacks' time had finally come and we were in charge of our own lives.

One time when I was in sixth grade, a rumor spread that a group of Black Panthers were coming to our school to save us from the evil white teachers. We were elated. We walked around with our chests pumped up, talking about the white teachers who hated us as much as we hated them. We told the white teachers that the Panthers were going to "get them" for making our lives miserable. We waited for weeks, but the Black Panthers never came to our school. No one came to deliver us. We were stuck in rural Mississippi and the outside world didn't even know we existed.

The Black Panther Party for Self-Defense was based in Oakland, California. It was founded in 1966 by Huey Newton and Bobby Seale as an offshoot of the Lowndes County Freedom Organization that SNCC workers had formed during a voter registration project in Alabama after the Selma-to-Montgomery march.

Party members in Oakland wore black berets, black leather jackets, and dark sunglasses and they carried weapons to defend themselves against police violence. They created chapters in major cities across the country. They believed in self-defense and black liberation. They provided blacks with protection against white police in black neighborhoods, provided free breakfasts to the needy, conducted voter registration drives, supported free health clinics, and established schools for black children. They also had many gun fights with police.

I was intrigued by the Black Panther Party because it did not believe in nonviolent protest as the only way to gain equality. No way was I going to allow white people to viciously beat me without defending myself.

The Black Power Movement brought out black consciousness in me like never before. For the first time in my life, the word "black" had a positive connotation. Before that, everything negative was black—Black Monday, black magic. Even today, I prefer to use black over African American because when it was coined, it carried so much power and authenticity.

Voting Campaign in Mississippi

Robert Moses of SNCC went to McComb, Mississippi, in the summer of 1961 to help register blacks to vote. He was a mathematics teacher from New York. He had helped establish the Freedom Schools, to teach voter literacy. Blacks in Walthall and Amite counties asked Moses and SNCC to establish Freedom Schools in their areas as well.

Whites reacted violently to the voter registration drives. A white state legislator shot and killed an Amite County man who was active in voter registration. A witness who the Justice Department failed to protect was beaten and later murdered after the FBI leaked information to a deputy sheriff.

Moses was arrested after bringing blacks to register. He was later beaten, but he filed charges against the man who beat him. A trial was held and the man was acquitted by an all-white jury.

Meanwhile in Jackson in 1961, students were causing their own civil disobedience. Nine black high school students who were members of the Tougaloo NAACP Youth Council participated in Mississippi's first civil rights "read-in" at the whites-only Jackson Municipal Public Library. On March 27, 1961, the "Tougaloo Nine" entered the library and refused a police order to leave. They were arrested and charged with breach of peace. They spent thirty-two hours in jail.

Jackson State College, which is now a university, held many student protests in the 1960s. In March 1961, Medgar Evers led a prayer meeting in front of the H. T. Sampson Library to protest the arrest of the Tougaloo Nine. Hundreds of students sang hymns, prayed, and shouted "We want freedom." Police officers arrived and ordered the students to disperse. The college administration threatened to expel them. The next day students boycotted classes and marched down J. R. Lynch Street toward the city jail. Police with clubs, dogs, and tear gas turned them around.

Two days later they went to court where the black section over-flowed with supporters of the students. When the nine demonstra-tors arrived at the courthouse, the crowd clapped and cheered. The police, again with clubs, dogs, and tear gas, attacked the supporters standing in front of the building. Many in the crowd, including Medgar Evers, were hurt. The Tougaloo Nine were found guilty of breach of peace and fined 100 dollars each. They received thirty-day suspended sentences for agreeing not to participate in future demonstrations.

Back in McComb, after the high school students were released from jail, some of them were not allowed to return to school. The others were asked to sign papers, declaring that they would not further participate in segregation demonstrations. When SNCC workers protested with a march on McComb's city hall, they were badly beaten. SNCC then opened its own high school.

In 1962, SNCC worked with the NAACP and COFO, a coalition of organizations that worked on civil rights. In April 1962, the Voter Education Project (VEP) was created to oversee voter registration work and manage the foundation money that the federal govern-ment provided. COFO distributed the money for VEP. But the hard part was convincing blacks in the rural South to register to vote.

In the summer of 1962 in Greenwood, Mississippi, VEP funded a voter registration project. At the time, only a small percentage of blacks were registered voters. Voter registration workers were threat-ened. At the end of the year, county officials fought back by voting to end participation in the federal commodities program, which sup-plied surplus food to the poor. So SNCC organized its own food drive and imported donated food from the North.

In early 1963, when some blacks tried to register at the courthouse in Greenwood, angry whites retaliated by burning black-owned businesses. The police arrested black leaders whom they considered troublemakers. Some of the black leaders were shot at. When more blacks tried to register, police allowed their dogs to attack them. The COFO office was set afire and black leaders sought federal protection for its registration workers. After many requests, the Justice Department went into federal court on March 31, 1963, to obtain a restraining order against local Mississippi officials. But the department ended up making a deal with those same officials: They would drop the injunction request if the officials stopped blacks from demonstrating.

VEP stopped funding voter registration campaigns in Mississippi in November 1963, because of the large amount of money spent there with few results. But that didn't stop unregistered blacks from trying to vote in primaries. They were turned away or arrested, but when a fall election was held, blacks participated in their own mock election.

The Right to Vote

Mama and Daddy thought the best way to fight oppression was by voting, and after President Johnson signed the Voting Rights Act of 1965 into law, they voted in every election. No matter how much cotton Daddy had in the field or how bad the weather was, they always drove to Pocahontas to vote. They voted for Democrats because they supposedly supported programs to help blacks.

Whites came to our church to campaign during election years, and the pastor allowed them time to speak during the service. Election years were one of the few times I saw white people in our church. After the election, I never saw them again. Granny said blacks were proud when Charles Evers, the brother of slain civil rights activist Medgar Evers, was first elected mayor of Fayette, Mississippi, in 1969. Evers was the first black mayor in the state since Reconstruction. I was familiar with the town of Fayette because our high school football team often played against the high school team there.

Back then, blacks spoke for the whole race. There was no such thing as a leader being simply a leader. There were white leaders and there were black leaders. Mama and Daddy knew that a black leader would speak for the rights of all blacks. Black people were black people. It didn't matter if you had 10 percent or 20 percent white blood, you were black. It didn't matter if your complexion was as light as Lena Horne's or as dark as Nat King Cole's.

When Thurgood Marshall, an attorney for the NAACP, argued cases before the U.S. Supreme Court, he represented all black people. And, when he became a justice on the U.S. Supreme Court in 1967, he continued to fight for us. Marshall was old and sickly but refused to retire from the high court until 1991. He waited until the nation elected a Democratic president, Bill Clinton, who would nominate a liberal justice to replace him. He didn't want to leave the disenfranchised without a voice. There was no such thing as, "I made it, you have to make it too." We were all in this together.

Forty years have changed all that. Clarence Thomas is a prime example of someone who got into college because of affirmative action, became a Supreme Court Justice because of affirmative action, and now speaks *against* affirmative action. He seems to have forgotten his Southern roots and the Jim Crow laws that kept him from the same things affirmative action opened up to him. Had it not been for blacks who lost their lives fighting for these things, Thomas would certainly not be a member of the highest court in the land. Some conservative whites admire Thomas because he thinks like they do, and they feel comfortable around him, but he doesn't represent the majority of black people in this country.

Affirmative Action

Affirmative action was introduced by President Johnson in 1965 to rectify centuries of racial discrimination because civil rights laws and constitutional amendments failed to protect blacks. Johnson implemented affirmative action so blacks and other minorities had a more level playing field in education and jobs when it came to promotions, salaries and career advancement, school admissions, and financial aid. Even college-educated blacks sometimes worked as bellboys and porters. The only decent respectable jobs open to blacks at that time were teaching positions at all-black schools.

For centuries, people of color were segregated into low-wage jobs, usually farming. I think about Daddy and how all he ever knew was farming because his father and grandfather were farmers. My brothers and sisters and I wanted to break that tradition.

We hated working in the fields. We wanted to do something we enjoyed, not something that was forced on us for generations.

Originally, the affirmative action law was enacted to make discrimination against minorities and women illegal. The law also stated that beneficiaries must have relevant and valid job or educational qualifications. But by the 1970s, whites started complaining about reverse discrimination. I couldn't believe it. After more than 300 years of white privilege, I wondered how they dared to start whining about reverse discrimination. For all these years, they had brutalized, oppressed, and castigated blacks; they had the nerve to complain. What about us? Blacks in the rural South were systematically banned from the very public facilities that they helped pay for with their taxes. Whites were willing to allow blacks to shop at their stores but not eat at their lunch counters. With Jim Crow laws, everything was separated by race. Your race defined you in the South—it defined where you lived and where you went to school; who you dated and who you married; where you ate and shopped.

Some white people will tell you that the flaws in affirmative action caused it to fail. They say that they were forced to hire people of color who were unqualified. In fact, the system had flaws because some employers hired blacks and set them up to fail.

During my first year as a reporter in 1989, I felt as though I was set up to fail and I didn't like that feeling. While working briefly at the *Los Angeles Times'* San Diego bureau, I was the only black reporter there. Late one afternoon, an editor sent me to Duluza, an isolated town in the mountains of San Diego County, to look for an elderly man whose dogs had mauled him to death. She sent me in the afternoon and it was probably a two-hour drive from the city. I arrived there and found a small café, the Dulzura Café, on the main road. Just like in the movies, it seemed like the piano music stopped when I walked in. All eyes were on me.

Someone said, "You must be lost." When I told the crowd I was a reporter for the *Los Angeles Times,* they said "Yeah, right." I asked around, but no one could tell me where to find the man with the raving mad dogs. When I called the bureau office and reported that I could not find the dog owner, another editor told me to get in my car, lock the doors, and get back to the office. I didn't know it at the time, but when several reporters found out that I had gone there alone, they chided the editors for sending me up into the mountains by myself. Usually, when a reporter goes into a dangerous area, two reporters or a reporter and photographer go together. When I arrived at the office that night, several reporters showed me newspaper clippings detailing how some white men had beaten a black man for trying to eat at the Dulzura Café. I thanked God for getting me out of there alive.

Affirmative action suffered a setback in 1978 when Allan Bakke, a white man, said he was rejected in two consecutive years by a medical school that he claimed accepted less qualified minority applicants. The school had reserved only sixteen out of one hundred places for minority students, but he wanted one of those sixteen. The Supreme Court ruled that affirmative action was legal, but it also ruled against inflexible quota systems in affirmative action programs, claiming that Bakke was unfairly discriminated against because he was white.

I was totally shocked by the Bakke ruling because, as a poor black child growing up in Mississippi, I didn't start off in life with a level playing field. The cards were stacked against me even before I was born. My school was inadequate. My education was inadequate. My parents' jobs were inadequate. Our sharecropper homes were inadequate. I was discriminated against all my life in Mississippi.

Jim Crow laws banned blacks from going to good schools. We were banned from good-paying jobs. We were banned from all the privileges in the great state of Mississippi. And now, when it was my time to go to college, the Supreme Court of the United States was telling me that I was not qualified to go to a so-called good school. The laws of my state had kept blacks oppressed, beaten down, and illiterate for more than 300 years, and now the highest court of the land was saying, "You're still not qualified to share in white privilege."

Mississippi schools hardly prepared me for the rigors of college. My only salvation was that I had read a lot growing up and had done well in English. When I was a teen, my oldest brother Jerry had given me books and insisted that I read the black classics because he said

Frankye visiting Mississippi while on college break in the early 1980s. Author's original family photograph.

they were essential to my understanding life as a black person in America.

When I left Mississippi in 1980 I went to Milwaukee to be with my older brothers and sisters who had left for the same reason—to find jobs. I lived with my sisters who helped support me while I finished college. I enrolled in a community college and planned to major in English or English literature because I wanted to spend the rest of my life writing novels. But Jerry talked me out of it. He said I needed to major in something that would pay off in a lucrative job once I left college.

I didn't care about making lots of money; I wanted a profession that I would enjoy and that included writing. I talked to an advisor who suggested that I take journalism. I wasn't interested in news reporting, mainly because I wasn't familiar with it. I also had no

Some of Frankye's family at their sister's Lillie's house in Milwaukee on Christmas Day in 1975. Back row (*left to right*): Ora (holding sister Martha's son Corey), Daddy, Lillie (holding sister Ora's daughter Valerie), and Daphne, Lillie's daughter. Author's original family photograph.

interest in politics and wanted to stay on the literary track. But there were few jobs for creative writing majors.

My advisor took me over to the school's student newspaper office and I signed up as a reporter. I knew little about journalism and felt out of place around the all-white staff, with whom I had nothing in common. I felt intimidated because the other staff members had experience and I sensed they had little patience for a novice reporter. I was expected to write critical news stories about school issues.

I wanted to run and hide behind my incompetence. What if I embarrassed myself? Instead of giving up, I went out and bought the local newspapers and studied them. I paid attention to how reporters crafted sentences, what information they included, and how they organized stories.

The more I wrote for the school paper, the better I got and the more I enjoyed the power of seeing my name in print. The next semester, I moved on to the University of Wisconsin—Milwaukee, a four-year college. It didn't have a journalism program, so I majored in mass communications, with an emphasis on journalism. I earned A's and B's in my writing classes. I went to the student newspaper and got a freelance writing job, which didn't pay much. Again the staff was all white, and although we got along fine, I didn't make friends with any of them. I kept hanging around because I needed the writing experience.

The next year, the black student union restarted its newspaper and I was hired as editor-in-chief. The paper was called *Invictus.* The work was draining, but the power I held was exhilarating. Unfortunately, we didn't get enough advertising to stay afloat and the paper went under again the next year.

In college, I went through more jobs than I care to remember. I worked in a hospital cafeteria, a bank, a laundry shop where I sorted and pressed work uniforms, and two neighborhood newspapers. I was never happy at any of those jobs. None of them was what

Frankye with her college roommates at a party at her brother Jerry's house in Milwaukee in the early 1980s. Author's original family photograph.

I wanted to do. All my life I wanted to be an artist but I never pursued formal training, partly because I knew I couldn't make a living drawing and painting and I didn't want to be a failure. I didn't leave Mississippi to fall flat on my face. It took me a few years to finish school because I worked, saved money for school, and attended classes until the money ran out. I worked second and third shifts, but they were hard on me. I also worked during spring break and tried not to be envious of the students who talked about going to Florida and frolicking on the beach for a week. When I finished college, I continued to work at newspapers. I started out at the *Los Angeles Times*.

The whole purpose of affirmative action was to break down the walls of segregation and oppression. Suddenly, whites, who finally felt the sting of discrimination, were building them back up in anger and revenge. In many cases where white applicants competed with black applicants for school admission or jobs, they sued if a black person was selected. Why? Did they assume they were better qualified simply because they were white? I don't recall many cases in which whites sued if they competed against other whites and lost. Maybe they assume white people are more qualified because of their race.

Although racist Southerners said that blacks were incapable of learning because their brains were smaller than those of whites, I beg to differ. Despite the horrible education I received in Mississippi, I persevered and worked very hard so that I could go to an affordable college. I was able to go to the college of my choice because the barriers of discrimination had been broken down, in part by affirmative action programs. If it wasn't for Martin King, Medgar Evers, James Meredith, Fannie Lou Hamer, members of the NAACP, SNCC, and SCLC, and the thousands of black people who were lynched or beaten and killed, I would still be a second-class citizen with no education.

Is this what George Wallace meant when he stood on the steps of the capitol and proclaimed, "Segregation now, segregation tomorrow, segregation forever"? Is this what angry white men wanted when they began a backlash against affirmative action? Is this America, the home of the free, as Fannie Lou Hamer asked when she went to the 1964 Democratic Convention to protest discrimination in the party that refused to let black people participate?

How can blacks compete without some sort of imposed equality? Blacks are not looking for a handout. We want the same things that any other American wants—the right to live in safe neighborhoods, the right to a good education, and the right to get paid the same salaries as white men. Affirmative action didn't fail; whites failed it because they didn't participate in it willingly. Their main excuse is, "We can't find anyone qualified." Well, where are you looking? If you're looking for an engineer, why would you go to a factory? Why wouldn't you check out engineering schools?

For many years whites had their own affirmative action. If they wanted to hire someone, they asked their friends or their colleagues who suggested their own family members or friends— "Just send that good ole' boy down here, I know his dad." And, if the person didn't know how to do the job, he was trained and given a mentor to work with. But after affirmative action was implemented, whites word-of-mouth affirmative action system no longer worked because their friends and colleagues didn't know any black people. That's what happens when races are segregated.

At the *Los Angeles Times*, I became good friends with a veteran reporter who told me never to speak badly about one reporter to another reporter because you never know who is married to whom. This was the best advice I received.

On my first day at the paper's San Diego bureau, I was told that one of the metro editors had said that a certain general assignment reporter, a white woman, "couldn't write her way out of a paper bag." Apparently, they had clashed many times when he edited her stories on deadline at night. But a few years down the road, her skills must have greatly improved because reportedly the two had an affair, the metro editor's wife kicked him out of the house, he moved in with the reporter who couldn't write, and two years later she was working on the downtown Los Angeles metro desk, the choice beat for any deserving reporter. Her lover, the editor, had also been promoted to the L.A. desk. I thought about how I had struggled as a young reporter to learn the ropes at a large newspaper. There was no white knight in shining armor to rescue me from covering the boring night meetings in small obscure towns.

Often in San Diego, I faced editors who were unapproachable on their best days. One time I was talking to Jonathan, a co-worker, about how rude the editors were and he said that they were busy and I should be selective about when and how I approached them. Well, I observed Jonathan and how he walked up any time he pleased to chitchat with the editors; they were all smiles with him. I learned later that Jonathan played poker with the men in the office, including the editors, on weekends. They had built a solid good-old-boy network. I don't play poker and have no intention of learning.

However, Times Mirror, which at the time owned the *Los Angeles Times*, did have the right idea about growing their own journalists of color. The eight-week intensive training program that brought me to Southern California was created to give budding minority reporters, editors, and photographers an opportunity that no one else was offering.

Although there were some reporters and editors who welcomed us and worked well with young reporters and photographers, there were many white journalists at the competitive paper who were not pleased by these METPRO's (Metropolitan Editorial Training Program), as we were called. Some falsely assumed that we were there to displace them. Others thought we were getting a free ride or didn't work hard enough to get the jobs. But we did work hard and we were held to higher standards just because of those feelings. We did not get preferential treatment, nor did I feel that I was filling a quota. I was a journalist, just like the other reporters.

During my first few weeks at the paper, I broke a front-page story about a man who had captured mostly Spanish-speaking women and held them as sex slaves in a beat-up camper in East Los Angeles. He had fathered many children with these women. He targeted them because he figured that if they escaped, they would be afraid to report the incident to authorities because they were illegal immigrants.

I was working the cop beat in a rough downtown precinct when a detective told me about the story and one victim in particular. My editor didn't believe me; he said that the woman had probably gotten mad at her boyfriend and made up the story. It was definitely not a *Los Angeles Times* story, he added. I knew the victim had not lied because I had talked two of my colleagues in the program who spoke Spanish into going with me to East L.A. to research the story, which turned out to be true. We talked to many people in the neighborhood who had seen the man with his captives and their children.

I bypassed my editor in the training program and went directly to the metro desk. When I related the story to one of the editors, she was so excited that she tried to take the story from me, but I fought to stay on it and work with the veteran reporters who spoke Spanish.

If given the opportunity, people of color can accomplish great things. Affirmative action was created for this reason. I hate being compared to other immigrants who came to this country and pulled themselves up by their bootstraps. After a few years of discrimination, white immigrants were eventually accepted into society as citizens. I have never felt that way. There are still some white people who believe that they are superior to blacks. How could I get over slavery when it was still present in the minds of Mississippians when I was growing up in the 1970s?

During the 1960s, blacks were still being lynched in the South. There were not many professional jobs for blacks in the 1970s. When you graduated high school, if you didn't go to college, you left the state. Why do conservatives think that blacks have come so far and America doesn't need affirmative action?

Over the years, I went to many journalism job fairs where newspaper recruiters refused to interview job seekers unless they had ten years' experience. Others would say the paper had no openings. I knew from these responses that these papers were not serious about wanting to hire journalists of color. When I left college, I knew that I needed experience at a newspaper to become a better journalist. I was good at writing college English papers, but news reporting is a whole different style of writing. Most college graduates face the same problem. No matter how well you do in college, you still need on-the-job training to succeed in the real world. For blacks, affirmative action was the only way to gain experience.

The arguments for and against affirmative action seem to be never ending. In 2003, the Supreme Court upheld the University of Michigan's affirmative action policies for its law school. But, it made the school change its undergraduate admissions program, which used a point system that rated students and awarded additional points to minorities.

Whenever the subject of affirmative action arises in workplaces, some whites never fail to include, "We want to hire the best qualified person for the job," as if blacks aren't qualified to work in leadership positions or corporate America. I do not demand that bosses hire unqualified blacks, but I do expect an even field for us to compete on, something I never had in Mississippi. Affirmative action isn't a bad thing, but sometimes people of color are hired to fill quotas and they receive no support afterward. They're like the black students who were bused to the white schools. If they fail, their bosses say affirmative action is flawed. Or they blame the black students or the employees.

An editor I befriended at the *Los Angeles Times* told me that when he was a reporter he resented it when journalists of color were promoted. He said that editors told him that it was because of affirmative action. He said he found out differently when he became an editor. The editors told white reporters that lie because they didn't want to tell them that they were not good enough to cover a certain beat.

After I finished the training program in 1990, the *Los Angeles Times* hired me to work at one of its bureaus in the San Gabriel Valley. I lived in Pasadena and covered a few towns in the surrounding area. One time I was at a meeting in San Dimas town hall. Before the town council meeting, the people stood up to salute the flag and say the Pledge of Allegiance. I sat in the reporter's box going over the council's agenda, making notes, and paying no attention to what was going on around me. Suddenly, I heard someone call my name. When I looked up, I realized it was the mayor asking me if I would like to join in. I politely declined. I thought nothing more of it because I had never joined in with them before and I wasn't there for that; my job was to report the news.

When I returned to work the next day, the senior editor in our bureau called me into her office and said the mayor called to say that I had disrupted their town meeting the night before. I was baffled because I had no idea what she was talking about. She told me that the mayor said I refused to stand up and salute the flag. My face began to feel hot. "The flag? The flag?" I asked her furiously. "I saluted that flag when I was in grade school because teachers made me, but I refuse to salute it now. That flag and everything it represents had taken away the rights that the Constitution guarantees me, and you want me to stand up and salute it?"

To be honest, when I was at the meeting, none of these things were going through my head. But when that editor, who was from a Southern state and who I considered a racist, demanded that I stand up and salute the flag whenever I covered that town, I blew a fuse. I have never been a militant, but I do believe in standing up for myself and not allowing people to push me around. I had been oppressed in Mississippi for too long to let this white woman make such demands on me.

She went on to say that if I didn't stand up and salute the flag, she would call the "higher ups" downtown. She picked up the phone and stared at me. I couldn't figure out what she was trying to do. Call my bluff? Then she asked, "So, are you going to stand up and salute the flag." I said no. Her face flushed. She couldn't understand why I wouldn't do it. She was just like other racist whites from the Deep South who thought blacks were happy singing out in those cotton and tobacco fields. They didn't know that blacks sang to cover their pain or to send messages to other blacks about secret meetings to fight for justice. How could I salute a flag that to me was a symbol of oppression, not the freedom it represented for whites? I could not bring myself to do it.

After some back and forth, I told her I was willing to go to the meetings and stand outside the door until the council finished saluting the flag. She agreed to that and hung up the phone. Now that I think back on it, I wish I had pushed her to call downtown so that I could defend myself, because after that my relationship with her went downhill. I felt extremely uncomfortable around her and we spoke to each other only when necessary. Not that we had been buddies before that, but things were different. I knew then that my days at the paper were numbered.

Although I enjoyed living in Southern California, I was happy to leave the paper. It had not been a good experience for me. I was ready for a new start, somewhere far away. I had come to Los Angeles right out of college, young and inexperienced, and it was the first of many battles I endured with white corporate America. It took me a while to learn how to play its political games, but it didn't take me long to realize that as long as blacks were cleaning white people's houses, babysitting their children, and cooking for them, they can tolerate us. But when we come into their corporations, some of them can't stand to see us do well.

I suppose I would be afraid, too, if after 300 years of privilege, I was no longer a part of the majority. Black people are usually the ones who have to integrate neighborhoods and jobs. White people don't like to leave their comfort zones; most of them are afraid to go into predominately black areas. As a reporter, I felt the same about going into all-white areas. But my editors didn't understand that. They saw whites as victims and blacks as aggressors. Having grown up in Klan-infested Mississippi, I have the opposite viewpoint.

Change Is Inevitable

At times, I cannot shake the anger I feel for the years I spent imprisoned in a world of racism and discrimination when I wasn't allowed to speak my mind. Often I remind myself that I can't go back and right a wrong that took place many years ago. I tell myself to go on with my life and stop living in the past, because change is inevitable, even in Mississippi where race relations have improved.

The 1980s brought change even to the neighborhood where I grew up. There used to be no white people living on our dirt road. Suddenly, houses popped up on the other side and white faces sat on the porches. They waved at us when we walked or drove by. I was astounded. The road was no longer made of rocks and sand—it was paved and called Pine Grove Road. Post office box numbers were upgraded to street addresses. Our small enclave was no longer exclusive. Thirty years ago, whites ran away from us. Now, they wanted to live near us, as neighbors.

Previously, the only white people who had set foot in our neighborhood and established relationships with us were a white preacher and his family. He conducted weekly Bible studies and a weeklong vacation Bible school each July at our church and at churches in several other black communities. We had Sunday school classes on the first and third Sundays of each month and church service on the second and fourth Sundays, so the white preacher came to our church on the first and third Sunday evenings.

We sang happy songs as opposed to the Negro Spirituals we sang during the regular church service. The preacher gave us "memory verses" to learn and we got points for memorizing them, answering Bible questions, and reciting the titles of all the books in the Bible. At the end of each class, we redeemed the points for candy that the white preacher brought in the trunk of his car. He used to throw candy out to us and we scrambled and fought over it until someone said

**Frankye's family's house in Mississippi in 1978. The house was built in 1970.
Author's original family photograph.**

that it was demeaning and he stopped tossing the candy in the air.

Blacks respected the white preacher because he was brave enough to come into our neighborhood. He had done this type of evangelizing for years. He did it when Daddy was a child and attended the classes. That's why Daddy made us go. We couldn't understand why the preacher kept coming, even after the Klan burned down his house several times. I used to think he came to black churches because whites didn't want him at their churches, but no one asked and he didn't volunteer a reason.

Everyone called him Reverend, even the adults, but he called all the blacks by their first names. As nice as the preacher seemed, I felt distant from him and his family. I thought he was mysterious. He didn't have a church or a regular job, but he had a house and two daughters. Each year, a man from up North brought the white preacher a brand new car. Because he didn't have a job, people were always giving him something. After a while we started holding appreciation programs and people came from all over with donations.

The white preacher liked telling us about miracles that happened in his life. His favorite was the time he and his wife and baby daughter went to the service station to buy gas. He only had two dollars and the baby needed milk, so he had to choose between buying gas and milk. He got both and the cashier, who didn't know the young preacher's predicament, refused to take his money. The preacher said this was truly a blessing from God. When he first told that story years ago, it made us speechless because we knew of no one who ever went to a store and got something without paying for it. We all agreed it was a miracle and began looking for similar blessings in our lives. I suppose just surviving Mississippi was a miracle in itself.

The only other whites we had contact with were the ones Mama worked for. Over the years, she worked for four families, two of them for more than twenty years. One of the families had two teenage girls and the mother used to give Mama their old clothes. I remember how excited we got when Mama brought home cardboard boxes bursting with dresses, sweaters, and shoes. Most of them weren't our sizes, but they looked expensive and had funny names on the labels. My sisters cut and sewed to make them fit.

Another family Mama worked for had three boys and they came over sometimes to play with my brothers or hunt with their father in the woods on Daddy's land. Mama never called the boys "mister," but they always said "ma'am" to her. Their mother also gave Mama boxes of clothes for us. One of the boys later attended and played football for Ole Miss, and in the boxes were white T-shirts and sweatshirts with the name of the school written in bold, red letters across the top and a picture of the mascot, a bulldog. I loved wearing T-shirts and sweatshirts to school, but I thought of James Meredith and what Ole Miss stood for, and I couldn't bring myself to wear these shirts in public. I didn't tell Mama why.

Mama sometimes took me with her to help clean. The houses of these white families looked like those in the magazines Mama brought home from work. I read every book and magazine she brought home. I dreamed of building a big house for mama like the ones I saw.

Mama deserved a house like those in the magazines.

Mississippi Today

In 1963, Galloway United Methodist Church in Jackson went against the national United Methodist Church when its church's board voted to prohibit blacks from worshiping at its church. That year, five African Americans tried to integrate the church and were turned away. The pastor, Dr. W. B. Selah, and associate minister Jerry Furr resigned in protest. Others were also turned away and some were arrested and put in jail for trying to attend services. But in 1966, the board changed its policy and allowed anyone to join.

In the 1960s, the Jackson headquarters for the YWCA was for whites only. But the YWCA's main office director and the director of the YWCA's branch for blacks eventually integrated the Jackson facility. The YWCA had its first black board member in 1967 and its first black president in 1974. I have friends in Jackson who have enrolled their children in the Y's summer programs.

In 1963, the Lawyers' Committee for Civil Rights Under Law, spearheaded by President Kennedy, was founded. The committee was a group of volunteer attorneys from all over the country who came to the state to represent people who could not get a lawyer to represent them in civil rights cases or could not afford to do so. When the committee first formed, there were only three civil rights attorneys in Mississippi to handle all the cases that were piling up in court. When the committee closed its Mississippi office in 1985, almost 200 black lawyers were practicing in the state.

Farish Street in Jackson was the place to be in the 1960s, but after years of neglect, it became a crime-infested area trafficked by male and female prostitutes. In 1980 it was listed on the National Register of Historic Places and in 1994 the city created the Farish Street Neighborhood Historic District. For the past two summers that I've visited, the area has been under renovation. It is being restored to its heyday. Major renovations were also going on at the Alamo Theater, which was the only theater in town where blacks could see a movie. It was the first theater I went to when I was a teenager. My cousins and I enjoyed going to see those horror movies and were so afraid to drive home afterward. Rural Mississippi is so dark at night that you can't see your hand in front of your face. When it's that dark, it's a long way from the car in the driveway to the front door.

Another change in Jackson is the city government. In the 1960s, there was a mayor and two commissioners. In the 1980s, voters changed it to a mayor/council type of government with city council members elected from individual wards. It was then that the first black city council members were elected. In 1997, Harvey Johnson, Jr. became the first black mayor of Jackson.

The house where Medgar Evers lived back then on Guynes Street was bought with a GI mortgage in 1957. The house was in a new subdivision that separated black and white neighborhoods. The street was renamed Margaret Walker Alexander Drive, after the Mississippi teacher, poet, and writer who wrote about the civil rights movement. She died in 1998. In 1994, the neighborhood was designated a Jackson Historic District. Evers' home is now a museum. It was donated to Tougaloo College, which oversees the property.

In the summer of 2003, my husband, son, and I went to see the house. The blood stains where Evers bled the night of his death are still on the driveway. It was eerie being there. While growing up, I had driven past that neighborhood hundreds of times and I never realized its significance. There is a saying in the South that when a murder occurs, the person's blood screams from the ground for justice. I didn't hear a sound that day in 2003. Justice had been served; Beckwith, Evers' killer, had died in prison.

The American Missionary Association founded Tougaloo College in 1869 on land that had been an antebellum cotton plantation. In 1998, the college was listed on the National Register of Historic Places. The private school and its administration, professors, and students wholeheartedly supported the civil rights movement in Jackson. Meetings, planning sessions, conferences, and rallies were held there.

Ghosts of Mississippi

The ghosts of Mississippi's segregated past came to rest in the 1990s. After more than thirty years, state prosecutors reopened some of the most horrific cases in which juries acquitted arrogant Klansmen who had senselessly murdered civil rights leaders.

On June 12, 1963, Byron De La Beckwith hid in some bushes and shot Medgar Evers in the back as he was standing in the driveway of his Jackson home with an armful of "Jim Crow Must Go" T-shirts. Evers had been at the New Jerusalem Baptist Church at a celebration that night after he led a day of picketing on Capitol Street on an injunction against demonstrations. Evers, thirty-seven, left behind a wife, Myrlie Evers, and three young children. In the 1990s, Myrlie served as national chairwoman of the NAACP.

Myrlie Evers never gave up the fight to convict her husband's killer. In 1989 she asked Bobby DeLaughter, the then-Assistant District Attorney of Hinds County to reopen the case. DeLaughter and his officers came across new evidence, including negatives of photos of the crime scene and new witnesses who testified that De La Beckwith admitted killing Evers. In the third and final trial, eight of the twelve jurors were black. De La Beckwith was convicted of murder in 1994. Beckwith appealed the conviction, but in 1997, the Mississippi Supreme Court upheld the decision.

Byron De La Beckwith, died at eighty while serving a life sentence in prison. He had been tried twice before in 1964 and both all-white juries deadlocked. It took the state thirty-one years to bring him to justice.

Sam Bowers, Imperial Wizard of the Mississippi White Knights of the Ku Klux Klan, was convicted in 1998 of conspiracy to commit the murder of civil right activist Vernon Dahmer. Bowers received a mandatory life sentence. The jury consisted of five blacks, six whites, and one Asian. In four previous trails, deadlocked juries could not agree on Bowers' guilt in the murder so judges declared them as mistrials. The Dahmer case was reopened when District Attorney Lindsay Carter, elected in 1995, uncovered new evidence that indicated jury tampering in Bowers' earlier trials. Vernon Dahmer, a father, businessman, and voting rights activist, was murdered

Statue of Medgar Evers. Photo by
Marc-Yves Regis I.

on January 10, 1966, the day after he announced that his black
neighbors could pay their poll tax at his store. His home was fire-
bombed during the early morning hours by three carloads of
Klansmen who pushed into the house and ignited twelve one-
gallon containers of gasoline. The house and adjacent store burned
to the ground. The back of the store was home to an elderly aunt.

Vernon and Ellie Dahmer and their youngest two children, Bettie
and Dennis, were awakened by the smoke and gunshots. The Dah-
mers' four older sons were serving in the military. Ellie Dahmer,
the children, and the aunt escaped the fire, but Vernon Dahmer
died twelve hours later from smoke inhalation and burns.

Sam Bowers and thirteen others were arrested on murder and
arson charges. Three were sentenced to life terms but they served less
than ten years. Another man was sentenced to ten years for arson but
he served only two.

Bowers also served six years in prison for his role in the 1964
killings of civil rights workers James Chaney, Andrew Goodman,

and Michael Schwerner. Bowers personally authorized the murder of "Goatee," the Klan's name for Schwerner. Bowers, then a thirty-nine-year-old businessman from Laurel, Mississippi, had established the White Knights of the Klu Klux Klan in the fall of 1963, and the white supremacy organization had about 10,000 members.

In 1989, after years of secrecy, the files of the Mississippi Sovereignty Commission were opened under court order. The commission had been created by the state legislature in 1956 to preserve Mississippi's legacy of segregation. The agency used tax money to spy on civil rights activists. The twenty-one-year court fight revealed the existence of more than 124,000 pages of secret files from a state agency that used intimidation, false imprisonment, jury tampering, and other illegal methods to stop the civil rights movement in the 1950s, 1960s, and early 1970s. Commission members wrote down the license plate numbers of cars parked at civil rights meetings and then looked into bank accounts to try and ruin the lives of the activists. The commission went out of business in 1977, after funding was cut. Lawmakers wanted the documents sealed until 2027, but a federal judge ordered them opened to the public in 1989.

I was very pleased to read about the reopening of the cases. Mississippi had finally become a part of the American society. But deep down, I was angry that it took more than three decades to bring justice to the families of the slain civil rights workers. Because the murderers walked free, these family members still lived in fear. Myrlie Evers left Mississippi and moved to California, I suppose to escape the ghosts in her head. I think I would have left too. How could you remain in a state where the leaders hate you and seek to kill you for demanding your civil rights? Many of these murderers were in their sixties and seventies and had enjoyed the best years of their lives in freedom. To me, a few years of incarceration before they died was hardly enough punishment. Over time I have gotten over my anger at Mississippi and its brutal oppression. Life goes on and my mental wounds have healed.

But some things never change. About five years ago my husband and I went to visit my parents in Mississippi and he wanted to photograph Philadelphia, where Chaney, Goodman, and Schwerner were murdered. When we got to the town, we first went to the police

From left to right: Frankye's brother Jerry, Daddy, Mama, her sister Martha, and Frankye at a 1994 family reunion in Mississippi. Photo by Marc-Yves Regis I.

station to get directions. The white police officer we talked to glanced around at the men in the station. "Why y'all want to see that place?" she asked. "It's on private property." But my husband persisted and she sent us off on a wild-goose chase. After about an hour of driving, we knew we were going in the wrong direction. We ended up in a nearby town and stopped and asked several people who claimed they had never heard of the dead men. Finally, we stopped at a business alongside the road and asked a man who was working outside. He told us that we needed to turn around and drive in the opposite direction. When we turned to leave, he added, "I never believed in all that stuff that went on," the old white man said. "It was wrong for them to kill those boys."

We thanked him and got back into the car and headed to our destination. When we got there, it was fenced in with a "No Trespassing" sign on the fence. You see a lot of these signs in Mississippi.

We stopped and talked to a black man sitting in his front yard. We told him we wanted to go the place where the volunteers had been buried. The man slowly looked up at us and said, "If I was ya'll, I would get back in my car and leave this place." This was enough for my husband. He burned rubber getting out of Philadelphia. On the way back to Jackson, I kept looking over my shoulder. We suspected that we were being followed and if any car stayed behind us for more than two minutes, we slowed down to let it pass.

I knew all too well about Southern white police officers following blacks on those long, dark country roads. Most of the time, those being followed were never heard from again.

Despite the glaring racism, when I visit Mississippi now, I can see the changes. My old middle/high school was torn down and rebuilt as a junior high school for white and black students. It was a county school when I attended, but when I called the school, the

Frankye wearing Mama's church hat in 1980. Author's original family photograph.

new principal told me that it has been incorporated into the Clinton Public School District in 1981. Wow! I thought to myself, this is twenty-seven years after the *Brown* decision banned segregation in public schools. When I was a student there, the school looked like a barn. The roof leaked and there was no air conditioning or heat. The bathrooms were filthy. However, before the white students were bused in, they made the building pristine. Some things in Mississippi never change.

Are blacks truly free in Mississippi? Well, when I go back to visit, it does feel like any other place I've lived in. Sure, things could be better, but I could also say that about any other place I've lived. Racism lives in the hearts and minds of people; it cannot be regulated. But I can truly say that when I go home to visit, I am "Free at last, free at last, thank God Almighty, I'm free at last."

Questions for Discussion and Reflection

Growing Up in Mississippi

1. Why were black people excluded from citizenship in this country? Discuss at least three reasons.

2. Imagine that you are part of a race of people who are not allowed equality in their country? What would you do?

3. Research lynching in the United States. How many black people were killed by this method and why?

4. Why did Frankye's family refuse to talk about the discrimination that black people faced in Mississippi? Did discrimination only occur in the South? Give other examples.

5. Frankye describes in detail her life growing up in Mississippi in the 1960s. Do you think white people lived similar lives? Try to find books and magazine or newspaper articles about how white people lived in the South in that era.

6. What were Jim Crow laws? What was their significance in maintaining segregation in the South? Did they work?

7. How did blacks manage to function under Jim Crow laws?

8. What types of relationship did black people have with whites? Did some whites live double lives? Explain.

9. What influence did racism have on Frankye's father's decision not to let her pursue a career in art? What damage did it do to her dreams?

10. What was the significance of skin color in the South and how did white people use it to divide the black race?

Early African-American History

1. When were Africans first brought to this country? Were they slaves? What happened to change their status in this country?

2. Use your imagination and describe how you would feel if you were kidnapped and crammed into a boat and shipped thousands of miles away to a foreign country. Discuss how it would feel to be sold as a slave to work in cotton and tobacco fields in 100- to 120-degree weather without pay.

3. Define abolitionist. How was the Abolitionist Movement beneficial to slaves?

4. Who was Dred Scot and why was the Supreme Court ruling in the *Dred Scott* decision important?

5. What caused the Civil War?

6. What was the Emancipation Proclamation? What did it do?

7. Did President Lincoln free the slaves because he was against slavery? Explain your answer.

8. Was the Reconstruction period helpful to black people? Why?

9. Name and define the three amendments to the Constitution that were implemented to bring justice to black people in America. Did they accomplish their goals? Explain.

10. How did racist Southern whites keep black people oppressed during the early twentieth century? What were Black Codes?

11. Who were some of the educated and prominent black people who fought against racism and discrimination? Give their names and discuss what they did in their struggle for equality.

12. What was the irony of black soldiers fighting in World War I and returning home to a society that considered them second-class citizens?

13. Why did the Black Nationalist movement fail?

14. Who were the Scottsboro Boys, and why did their case galvanize black people?

15. What role did communism play in the civil rights movement?

The Modern Civil Rights Movement

1. What was the significance of *Brown v. Board of Education* and why did it take so long for the courts to outlaw segregation?

2. What did white Southerners do to reverse the *Brown* decision?

3. How did Frankye's grandmother deal with the violence from hate groups in Mississippi?

4. How did the U.S. government conspire with white Southerners to keep blacks oppressed?

5. Why was the Montgomery bus boycott able to mobilize the black community when other mass movements had failed?

6. What happened when black students began to desegregate all-white schools in the South?

7. What role did the Kennedy Administration play in school integration?

8. What were Freedom Rides and how did they break down the walls of racial segregation?

9. Did the support of white people hurt or help black people's struggle for equal rights that were already guaranteed under the Constitution?

10. Did civil rights leaders' method of direct action succeed in Albany, Georgia? Why?

11. Why were officials in Birmingham, Alabama, allowed to disregard federal authority and bomb nonviolent black demonstrators without recourse?

12. Did the 1963 March on Washington change the educational and economic situation for black people? How?

My Schools

1. Describe how schools for black and white students differed in Mississippi in the 1960s and 1970s.

2. Do you think integration improved the educational opportunities for black students? Give details.

Sit-Ins

1. What were sit-ins and how were they important to the civil rights movement?

2. How did the civil right struggle affect presidential campaigns?

Equal Treatment

1. Why was Mississippi called a closed society? Was it more segregated than other Southern states? Explain.

2. How do you think segregation, racism, and discrimination affected the author? Give several examples.

Freedom Summer

1. What was Freedom Summer? Why was it conducted in Mississippi?

2. If the three civil rights workers had not been assassinated, how might the civil rights movement been different? Discuss.

3. Should the Mississippi Freedom Democratic Party have been allowed to represent the state at the 1964 Democratic Convention instead of the all-white racist Democratic slate of delegates? Explain.

4. Define COINTELPRO. What role did it play in discrediting the civil rights movement?

Voting Rights Struggle

1. What was Bloody Sunday and how did it propel Americans to get involved in the civil rights struggle?

2. Did the Voting Rights Act of 1965 pave an easy road for black people to flood the election booths? Explain your answer.

3. What change did young civil rights leaders make in the mid-1960s. Why?

Black Nationalism and Black Power

1. What contributions did black people in Mississippi make to voting rights in that state?

2. Define affirmative action and explain why it was created? Was it successful?

3. Was the author a beneficiary of affirmative action? Give examples.

Voting Campaign in Mississippi

1. Define what you think the author means by the term "Black Power." Did it help or hurt the continuing civil rights struggle?

2. Do you think that violence against black people in the 1960s has transformed into police brutality in the modern age?

3. Were black nationalist groups effective in gaining equality? Why?

Change Is Inevitable

1. How has the South changed to become a better place to live for black people?

Organizations

Council of Federated Organizations (COFO)

Congress of Racial Equality (CORE)

Equal Employment Opportunity Commission (EEOC)

Federal Bureau of Investigation (FBI)

Jackson Nonviolent Movement (JNM)

Ku Klux Klan (KKK)

International Labor Defense (ILD)

Interstate Commerce Commission (ICC)

Mississippi Freedom Democratic Party (MFDP)

National Association for the Advancement of Colored People (NAACP)

National Urban League

Southern Christian Leadership Conference (SCLC)

Student Nonviolent Coordinating Committee (SNCC)

Universal Improvement Association (UNIA)

Voter Education Project (VEP)

Glossary

Abernathy, Ralph. The pastor of the First Baptist Church in Montgomery. He was second in command of the Southern Christian Leadership Conference (SCLC).

Abolitionists. People who fought to abolish slavery.

Albany Movement. The seat of white resistance in the South where the Student Nonviolent Coordinating Committee (SNCC) began a voter registration drive. Civil rights leader Martin Luther King, Jr. was arrested and jailed there. After numerous nonviolent demonstrations, the city refused to desegregate.

Asafetida. A gum resin from various Asiatic plants of the parsley family. It was used as a medicine to treat sickness, such as stomach aches.

Bakke, Allan. The first white person who won a reverse discrimination lawsuit. He won for failing to enter a medical school of his choice.

Barnett, Ross. The segregationist Mississippi governor from 1960 to 1964 who tried to block James Meredith, a black man, from entering the University of Mississippi.

Beckwith, Byron De La. A KKK member who was convicted in 1994 of assassinating Mississippi civil rights leader, Medgar Evers, in 1963. He was acquitted twice in the 1960s. It took the state thirty-one years to bring him to justice.

Bill of Rights. The first ten amendments to the Constitution.

Black Codes.   Laws created to keep blacks segregated, including a ban on mixed marriages and laws dictating that black people had to work for white people and they could not testify against them.

Black Panthers.   A black militant group that formed in 1966.

Bloody Sunday.   The day on which demonstrators marching from Selma to Montgomery, Alabama, were viciously beaten by police. The fifty-mile walk on March 7, 1965, ended at the Edmund Pettus Bridge.

Breaking verbs.   Using the wrong verb tense.

Brown v. Board of Education.   The Supreme Court decision that banned segregated schools on May 17, 1954.

Bowers, Sam.   The Imperial Wizard of the Mississippi KKK who ordered the murder of Vernon Dahmer, a prominent civil rights leader in the state. He was also involved in the murder of the three civil rights workers in Mississippi in 1964 during Freedom Summer.

Citizens Council (or White Citizens Councils).   A racist organization that formed on July 11, 1954, in Indianola in the Mississippi Delta. It consisted of business and professional whites. Chapters spread throughout the state and ruled it until 1963.

Civil rights.   Rights guaranteed citizens under the U.S. Constitution.

COINTELPRO.   Code name for a secret and illegal FBI operation that spied on citizens, especially during the civil rights struggle. These domestic counterintelligence programs ran from 1956 to 1971.

Congress of Racial Equality (CORE).   A civil rights organization that started the Freedom Rides through the South in 1961.

Connor, Eugene "Bull".   Public safety commissioner of Birmingham, Alabama, who was notorious for using violence to suppress nonviolent demonstrations against segregation.

Council of Federated Organization (COFO).   An umbrella group that helped Southerners register to vote.

Dahmer, Vernon.   A civil rights activist who was murdered at age thirty-seven in 1966 on the orders of Sam Bowers, Imperial Wizard of the Mississippi KKK.

De Facto Segregation. Segregation of races that occurs by choice or naturally, particularly in neighborhoods, rather than because of law.

Du Bois, W.E.B. A Harvard-educated black intellectual who was born into freedom in the North in 1868. He is known for his works, *The Souls of Black Folk* and *Up from Slavery,* an autobiography.

Emancipation Proclamation. President Lincoln's order in September 1862, which became effective January 1, 1863, that freed all slaves in territories still at war with the Union.

Evers, Medgar. Mississippi NAACP state field secretary and civil rights leader who was murdered in 1963.

Freedmen's Bureau. A federal agency set up during Reconstruction to help slaves get land.

Freedom Riders. A group of black and white students who integrated interstate buses and rode them through the South in 1961.

Freedom Schools. Schools created by volunteers who went to Mississippi to help register black people to vote. During the day, volunteers taught reading, writing, math, and black history. At night, the schools were used for political meetings.

Garvey, Marcus. A black leader from Jamaica who came to America in 1916. In 1919, he founded the Universal Improvement Association (UNIA) and promoted a back-to-Africa movement, urging black people to reject white society.

Hamer, Fannie Lou. A sharecropper from Ruleville, Mississippi, who spoke at the 1964 national Democratic Convention in Atlantic City, New Jersey. She attended with the delegation that represented the Mississippi Freedom Democratic Party, which asked to be seated instead of the state's all-white delegation. The state's Democratic Party had refused to allow black people to join.

Hoover, J. Edgar. Director of the Federal Bureau of Investigation (FBI) from 1924 to 1972, when he died. He was born in 1895.

Humphrey, Hubert H. Vice president of the United States from 1965 to 1969. He was born in 1911 and died in 1978.

International Labor Defense (ILD). A group controlled by the Communist Party.

Interstate Commerce Commission (ICC). A federal commission created in 1887 to regulate commerce between the states. The President appoints the eleven-member commission.

Jackson Nonviolent Movement (JNM). An offshoot of the Student Nonviolent Coordinating Committee (SNCC) that coordinated housing for Freedom Riders in Mississippi.

Jim Crow laws. Segregation laws that prohibited black people from using public facilities that served whites.

Johnson, James Weldon. A lawyer, journalist, author, and songwriter who wrote the Negro National Anthem, "Lift Every Voice and Sing."

Johnson, Lyndon B. The thirty-sixth president of the United States. He served from 1963 until 1969. He was born in 1908 and died in 1973.

Kennedy, John Fitzgerald. The thirty-fifth president of the United States. He served from 1961 until 1963, when he was assassinated. He was born in 1917.

Kennedy, Robert. Brother of President John F. Kennedy who served as attorney general in his administration.

King, Martin Luther. The leader of the civil rights movement. He also headed the Southern Christian Leadership Conference (SCLC).

Ku Klux Klan (KKK). A white racist terrorist organization founded after the Civil War to preserve white supremacy.

Lewis, John. A U.S. representative from Georgia who was a Student Nonviolent Coordinating Committee (SNCC) leader and an ordained Baptist minister.

Malcolm X. Charismatic Nation of Islam leader who promoted black separatism in the 1960s.

Marshall, Thurgood. NAACP attorney who later became a U.S. Supreme Court justice. He won the *Brown v. Board of Education* case in 1954. He was born in 1908 and was elected to the Supreme Court in 1967.

Memory verses. Biblical verses to memorize.

Meredith, James. The first black student to enroll in the University of Mississippi (Ole Miss).

Mississippi Freedom Democratic Party (MFDP). A political party organized to challenge the all-white Mississippi delegation to the national Democratic Party's 1964 convention in Atlantic City, New Jersey. Both blacks and whites were members. The party elected a slate of delegates to attend the convention and asked to be seated as the Democratic constitutional body of Mississippi. They were turned away.

Mississippi Sovereignty Commission. A commission created by the Mississippi legislature in 1956 to preserve the state's legacy of segregation.

Moses, Robert. A Student Nonviolent Coordinating Committee (SNCC) member from New York who went to Mississippi in the summer of 1961 to help black people register to vote.

Muhammad, Elijah. One of the leaders of the Nation of Islam, a Black Muslim organization.

Nation of Islam. A black Muslim organization founded in 1930.

National Association for the Advancement of Colored People (NAACP). An organization formed in 1909 to fight for the civil rights of black people and to put an end to lynching.

National Urban League. An organization formed in 1911 to help black people, who had migrated from the rural South, adjust to urban life in the North.

Parks, Rosa. A seamstress from Montgomery, Alabama, who is considered the mother of the modern civil rights movement.

Plessy v. Ferguson. A case brought before the Supreme Court by a black man, Homer Plessy, who was arrested in 1896 for riding in a railroad car reserved for whites. The Court ruled that states had the right to provide "separate but equal" facilities for blacks and whites.

Randolph, Philip A. President of the Brotherhood of Sleeping Car Porters who threatened a march on Washington, D.C., in 1941 unless President Roosevelt ended racial discrimination in the defense program.

Ray, James Earl. The man convicted and sentenced to ninety-nine years in prison for killing Martin Luther King. He died in prison in 1998.

Reconstruction. The years after the Civil War, from about 1867 to 1877, when the federal government reorganized the Southern states and established them in the Union.

Robeson, Paul. A communist sympathizer and an international star who starred in *Othello* on stage in London, sang "Ol' Man River" in *Showboat,* and starred in the movie *The Emperor Jones.*

Roosevelt, Franklin Delano. The thirty-second president of the United States who served from 1933 to 1945, the year he died. He was born in 1882.

Scottsboro Boys. Nine black youths, ranging in age from twelve to nineteen, who were accused of raping a white woman on board a freight train. Eight were sentenced to death. The verdicts were later reduced to prison terms.

"Separate but equal." Separate public facilities for whites and blacks that were supposed to be equal in quality.

Sharecropping. A system whereby tenant farmers planted and harvested crops on the white landowner's property so that they could get half of the yield.

Slop jar. Night potty.

Smith v. Allwright. A Supreme Court case in 1944 that banned the white primary, which had kept black people from voting.

Southern Christian Leadership Conference (SCLC). An Atlanta-based civil rights organization formed by a group of mostly Southern black ministers after the success of the Montgomery boycott. Martin Luther King was chosen to lead the organization in its fight to end segregation and help earn black people the right to vote.

Student Nonviolent Coordinating Committee (SNCC). A student organization that formed after the successful sit-ins in Nashville, Tennessee, in the early 1960s.

Take up. Buying merchandise on credit.

Thurmond, Strom. Long-time South Carolina senator who tried to reverse the *Brown* decision. In 1948, he ran for president on a platform of racial segregation.

Till, Emmett. A fourteen-year-old black boy from Chicago who was murdered and mutilated while visiting relatives in Mississippi. He allegedly whistled or said "Bye baby" to a white woman as he left a country store.

Tougaloo Nine.   Nine high school students and members of the Tougaloo NAACP Youth Council who went to the whites-only Jackson Municipal Public Library on March 27, 1961, and refused to leave. They were arrested and charged with breach of peace.

Universal Improvement Association (UNIA).   An organization established by Marcus Garvey in 1919 to support black separatism.

Voter Education Project (VEP).   An organization created to oversee voter registration work and manage the foundation money that the federal government provided. The Council of Federated Organization (COFO) distributed the money for VEP.

Wallace, George.   The Alabama governor who in January 1963 stood on the steps of the capitol and delivered his inaugural speech. To a cheering crowd, he yelled, "Segregation now, segregation tomorrow, segregation forever."

Washington, Booker T.   Born in 1856, the black author and educator founded Tuskegee Institute in Alabama.

Wells, Ida B.   A prominent black teacher and outspoken journalist who was born a slave during the Civil War. She condemned the lynching of blacks and spurred an international debate on the subject.

Sources

Branch, Taylor. *Pillar of Fire: America in the King Years 1963–65.* New York: Simon & Schuster, 1998.

Eyes on the Prize: American Civil Rights Years 1954 to 1965, vols. 1–6. PBS Home Video, 1995.

Fairclough, Adam. *Better Day Coming: Blacks and Equality. 1890–2000.* New York: Viking, Penguin Group, 2001.

"Jackson Civil Rights Movement Driving Tour Brochure." City of Jackson and the Jackson Convention and Visitors Bureau, November 2001.

Lucas, Eileen. *Civil Rights: The Long Struggle.* Springfield, NY: Enslow Publishers, 1996.

Powledge, Fred. *Free At Last? The Civil Rights Movement and the People Who Made It.* Boston, Toronto, London: Little, Brown, 1991.

Winters, Paul A., ed. *The Civil Rights Movement.* San Diego: Greenhaven, 2000.

Index

About the Author

FRANKYE REGIS is a freelance writer and editor. She has been a reporter and columnist for the *New Haven Register*, Cox Newspapers/Washington, D.C., Bureau, and the *Los Angeles Times*.